# Mexico Travel Guide

AVERY B. HODGES

Published by Travel The World, 2023.

MEXICO TRAVEL GUIDE

**First edition. October 3, 2023.**

Copyright © 2023 AVERY B. HODGES.

ISBN: 979-8223527121

Written by AVERY B. HODGES.

The information contained in this book is intended solely for informational purposes and general guidance. While every effort has been made to ensure the accuracy and reliability of the information presented, the author and publisher make no representations or warranties of any kind, express or implied, regarding the completeness, accuracy, or suitability of this information for any particular purpose.

The author and publisher disclaim any responsibility for any inaccuracies, errors, or omissions in this book and shall not be held liable for any consequences, including but not limited to personal injury, loss, or damage, resulting from reliance on the information presented herein. The reader assumes full responsibility for any decisions or actions taken based on the content of this book.

Security, travel regulations, and related matters are subject to change, often without notice. Readers are strongly encouraged to independently verify the information provided in this book and to stay updated on current security conditions, travel advisories, and legal requirements by consulting with relevant government authorities, official websites, and other reputable sources.

By reading this book, you acknowledge and accept the terms of this disclaimer and agree to use the information provided at your own risk.

# Chapter 1: Introduction to Mexico

Mexico, a vibrant and diverse country located in the southern part of North America, is a land of rich history, captivating culture, breathtaking landscapes, and warm-hearted people. This chapter aims to provide you with a brief overview of Mexico, encompassing its geography, history, culture, and the myriad of attractions that make it a must-visit destination.

Geography:

Stretching over 1,964,375 square kilometers, Mexico is bordered by the United States to the north and Belize and Guatemala to the south. Its extensive coastline runs along the Pacific Ocean to the west and the Gulf of Mexico and Caribbean Sea to the east. The country's diverse topography ranges from stunning beaches and lush jungles to towering mountains and expansive deserts, making it a geographical wonderland.

History:

Mexico boasts a rich and ancient history that dates back thousands of years. Before the arrival of the Spanish conquistadors in the 16th century, the region was inhabited by advanced civilizations such as the Aztecs, Mayans, and Olmecs. These civilizations left behind awe-inspiring archaeological sites, including the magnificent pyramids of Teotihuacan and Chichen Itza, which continue to amaze visitors to this day. The colonial period under Spanish rule greatly influenced Mexico's culture, architecture, and traditions, creating a unique blend of indigenous and European heritage.

Culture:

Mexican culture is a vibrant tapestry woven with a fusion of indigenous, Spanish, and modern influences. The warmth and hospitality of the Mexican people are renowned worldwide, making visitors feel welcome and embraced. The country's cultural heritage is celebrated through colorful festivals, traditional music, and dance, such as the lively Mariachi bands and the exuberant folkloric ballet. Mexican cuisine, recognized as an Intangible Cultural Heritage by UNESCO, tantalizes taste buds with its bold flavors and diverse regional dishes, such as tacos, enchiladas, and mole.

Attractions:

Mexico offers an abundance of attractions that cater to every traveler's taste. From the bustling capital city of Mexico City, with its historic center and world-class museums like the National Museum of Anthropology, to the stunning beach resorts of Cancun and Playa del Carmen along the Riviera Maya, there is something for everyone. Nature enthusiasts can explore the breathtaking Copper Canyon, go whale-watching in Baja California, or marvel at the unique biosphere reserve of Sian Ka'an. For history buffs, a visit to the ancient ruins of Palenque or the colonial cities of Guanajuato and Oaxaca is a must.

As you embark on your journey through Mexico, allow yourself to be captivated by its enchanting landscapes, immersed in its rich history, and embraced by its warm culture. With its diverse attractions and hospitable people, Mexico promises an unforgettable experience that will leave you yearning to return time and time again.

Remember, this is just a glimpse into the wonders that await you in Mexico. Each chapter of this guide will delve deeper into specific regions and attractions, providing you with a comprehensive understanding of this captivating country. So, get ready to embark on an adventure that will leave you with memories that will last a lifetime.,

# Chapter 2: When to Visit Mexico

Mexico, a land of vibrant culture, ancient ruins, and breathtaking landscapes, offers a plethora of experiences for every traveler. However, planning the perfect time to visit this diverse country can be a daunting task. In this chapter, we will provide you with insightful tips and guidance to help you determine the best time to embark on your Mexican adventure.

1. Weather Considerations:

Mexico's vast size and geographical diversity result in varying climates across different regions. It is crucial to consider the weather conditions when planning your visit. The country can be broadly divided into three climate zones: tropical, temperate, and arid.

a) Tropical Zone (Yucatan Peninsula, Riviera Maya, and Cancun): If you dream of exploring the stunning beaches and ancient Mayan ruins, the dry season from November to April is ideal. However, be prepared for higher prices and larger crowds during this period. The rainy season from May to October offers lush greenery and fewer tourists, but occasional downpours may interrupt your plans.

b) Temperate Zone (Mexico City, Guadalajara, and Oaxaca): These regions experience a more moderate climate. The dry season from November to April is considered the best time to visit, with pleasant temperatures and clear skies. The rainy season from May to October brings cooler temperatures, but also occasional showers. If you don't mind the rain, visiting during this season can provide a unique and authentic experience, as the landscapes come alive with vibrant colors.

c) Arid Zone (Baja California and Northern Mexico): The desert landscapes of Baja California and Northern Mexico offer a unique charm. The best time to visit is during the winter months (November to April) when temperatures are milder. Summers can be scorching hot, so it's advisable to avoid this period unless you are prepared for extreme heat.

2. Cultural Festivals:

Mexico is renowned for its vibrant festivals and cultural celebrations. If immersing yourself in the local traditions and festivities is high on your list, planning your trip around these events can enhance your experience. Some notable festivals include:

a) Day of the Dead (Día de los Muertos): Celebrated on November 1st and 2nd, this festival honors deceased loved ones. Oaxaca and Mexico City are particularly famous for their elaborate celebrations.

b) Guelaguetza: Held in Oaxaca during July, this festival showcases the state's indigenous cultures through traditional dances, music, and food.

c) Semana Santa (Holy Week): Taking place in the week leading up to Easter, Semana Santa is celebrated throughout Mexico with processions, religious ceremonies, and vibrant street decorations.

3. Budget Considerations:

Another crucial factor to consider when planning your visit to Mexico is your budget. Prices for accommodation, flights, and attractions can vary depending on the season. High season (November to April) generally sees higher prices due to increased demand. If you are traveling on a budget, consider visiting during the shoulder seasons (May to June and September to October) when prices tend to be more affordable.

In conclusion, Mexico offers a wealth of experiences throughout the year. By considering the weather, cultural festivals, and your budget, you can determine the best time to visit this enchanting country. Whether you are seeking sunny beach days, cultural immersion, or a mix of both, Mexico will undoubtedly leave a lasting impression on your travel memories.,

# Chapter 3: What to Pack for Your Trip to Mexico

Introduction:

As you embark on your journey to Mexico, it is essential to pack wisely to ensure a comfortable and enjoyable experience. This chapter will guide you through the necessary items to bring along, taking into consideration the diverse landscapes, climates, and cultural aspects of this vibrant country. From the sunny beaches of Cancun to the charming colonial towns of Guanajuato, let's explore what you should pack for your trip to Mexico.

1. Clothing:

Mexico's climate varies greatly depending on the region and time of year. When packing clothes, it is essential to consider the activities you plan to engage in and the weather conditions you may encounter. Here is a list of clothing items to consider:

- Lightweight and breathable clothing: Pack loose-fitting and breathable clothes made from natural fabrics like cotton or linen to stay cool in Mexico's tropical regions.

- Swimwear: Don't forget your swimsuit as Mexico boasts stunning beaches and crystal-clear waters.

- Comfortable walking shoes: Mexico's cities and towns are best explored on foot, so bring comfortable shoes suitable for walking.

- Sun protection: Pack a wide-brimmed hat, sunglasses, and sunscreen to shield yourself from the sun's rays.

- Layers: In mountainous regions or during cooler months, pack a light jacket or sweater for chilly evenings.

2. Essential Documents:

To ensure a smooth trip, it is crucial to have all the necessary documents readily available. Here are the essential documents to pack:

- Valid passport: Ensure your passport has at least six months of validity remaining from your planned departure date.

- Mexican Tourist Card (FMM): This document is typically provided by airlines or at the point of entry. Keep it safe throughout your trip.

- Travel insurance: Consider purchasing travel insurance that covers medical emergencies, trip cancellations, and lost belongings.

- Copies of important documents: Make copies of your passport, FMM, travel insurance, and other essential documents. Keep them separate from the originals.

3. Health and Safety:

Maintaining good health and safety practices is crucial when traveling to any destination. Here are some items to include in your packing list:

- Medications: If you take prescription medications, ensure you have an adequate supply for the duration of your trip. Additionally, pack a basic first aid kit with essentials like band-aids, pain relievers, and any personal medications you may need.

- Insect repellent: Protect yourself from mosquitoes and other insects by packing a reliable insect repellent.

- Hand sanitizer: Keep a small bottle of hand sanitizer with you for situations where soap and water may not be readily available.

- Portable water bottle: Staying hydrated is essential, so having a portable water bottle will come in handy, especially in areas where tap water is not recommended for drinking.

4. Miscellaneous Items:

In addition to the essentials mentioned above, consider packing these useful items:

- Power adapter: Mexico uses Type A and Type B sockets, so bring a power adapter if your devices have different plug types.

- Spanish phrasebook: While many Mexicans speak English, having a basic Spanish phrasebook can help you navigate conversations and immerse yourself in the local culture.

- Daypack or backpack: A small bag for day trips will allow you to carry your essentials comfortably.

- Camera or smartphone: Capture the beauty of Mexico by bringing a camera or smartphone to document your adventures.

Conclusion:

Packing appropriately for your trip to Mexico will ensure you have everything you need to fully enjoy this diverse and captivating country. Remember to consider the climate, activities, and cultural aspects of your destination when selecting what to pack. By following this guide, you'll be well-prepared to make the most of your Mexican adventure. ¡Buen viaje!,

# Chapter 4: Geography and Climate of Mexico

Introduction:

Welcome to Chapter 4 of our tourist guide to Mexico! In this chapter, we will explore the diverse and captivating geography and climate of this beautiful country. From its towering mountains to its stunning coastline, Mexico offers a wide range of landscapes that are sure to leave you in awe. Additionally, we will delve into the various climates you can expect to encounter during your visit, ensuring that you are well-prepared for your Mexican adventure.

1. The Physical Geography:

Mexico is blessed with a rich and varied physical geography that boasts an array of natural wonders. Let's take a closer look at some of the key features that define the landscape of this enchanting country.

1.1 Mountains:

Mexico is home to several magnificent mountain ranges, each with its own unique charm. The Sierra Madre Occidental, located in the northwest, stretches over 1,500 miles and offers breathtaking views and opportunities for outdoor exploration. The Sierra Madre Oriental, situated in the east, is known for its lush vegetation and diverse wildlife. Lastly, the Trans-Mexican Volcanic Belt, running across central Mexico, showcases stunning volcanic peaks, including the iconic Popocatepetl and Iztaccihuatl.

1.2 Rivers and Lakes:

Mexico boasts an extensive network of rivers and lakes, providing both scenic beauty and valuable resources. The Rio Grande, forming a natural border between Mexico and the United States, is the country's longest river. Other notable rivers include the Usumacinta, Grijalva, and Balsas. As for lakes, Lake Chapala, the largest in Mexico, is a popular destination for fishing and water sports, while Lake Texcoco, although mostly drained, holds historical significance as the former home of the Aztec capital, Tenochtitlan.

1.3 Coastline:

Mexico's coastline stretches for approximately 9,330 kilometers, offering a paradise for beach lovers and water enthusiasts. From the turquoise waters of the Caribbean Sea on the eastern coast to the rugged cliffs and Pacific swells on the western coast, Mexico's beaches cater to all tastes. Notable coastal destinations include Cancun, Playa del Carmen, Puerto Vallarta, and Acapulco, each with its own distinct charm and attractions.

2. The Climate:

Mexico's climate is as diverse as its geography, with a range of climatic zones that vary from region to region. Understanding the climate of the areas you plan to visit is essential for making the most of your trip. Let's explore the different climates you can expect in Mexico.

2.1 Tropical Climate:

The coastal regions of Mexico, particularly those along the Caribbean Sea and the Gulf of Mexico, experience a tropical climate. Expect high temperatures year-round, with relatively high humidity and the possibility of occasional rainfall. This climate is perfect for those seeking a sun-soaked beach vacation.

2.2 Arid and Semi-Arid Climate:

The northern regions of Mexico, including parts of Baja California and the states bordering the United States, have an arid or semi-arid climate. These areas receive limited rainfall and can experience scorching temperatures during the summer months. It is advisable to pack sunscreen, hats, and lightweight, breathable clothing when visiting these regions.

2.3 Temperate Climate:

In central Mexico, including Mexico City and surrounding areas, a temperate climate prevails. Mild temperatures and moderate rainfall characterize this region. Be prepared for cooler evenings, especially at higher elevations, and consider packing a light jacket or sweater.

2.4 Alpine Climate:

At higher elevations, such as in the mountainous regions of central and northern Mexico, an alpine climate dominates. Expect colder temperatures, especially during the winter months, and be prepared for the possibility of snowfall. Warm clothing, including hats and gloves, is essential for those venturing into these areas.

Conclusion:

As you can see, Mexico's geography and climate offer a remarkable tapestry of landscapes and weather conditions. From its majestic mountains and winding rivers to its stunning coastline and diverse climates, Mexico truly has something for every traveler. By understanding the geography and climate of the regions you plan to explore, you can ensure that your Mexican adventure is both enjoyable and memorable. So, pack your bags and get ready to immerse yourself in the natural wonders that await you in Mexico!,

# Chapter 5: The Regions of Mexico

Introduction:

Mexico, a country rich in culture, history, and natural beauty, is divided into several distinct regions, each with its own unique characteristics. From the vibrant cities to the serene coastlines and captivating landscapes, exploring Mexico's diverse regions promises an unforgettable experience. In this chapter, we will delve into the different regions of Mexico, highlighting their distinctive features and attractions.

1. The Yucatán Peninsula:

The Yucatán Peninsula, located in southeastern Mexico, is renowned for its ancient Mayan ruins, crystal-clear cenotes, and stunning Caribbean beaches. The region's crown jewel is Chichen Itza, one of the New Seven Wonders of the World, where visitors can immerse themselves in the fascinating history of the Mayan civilization. Additionally, the vibrant city of Mérida offers a blend of colonial and Mayan culture, while the coastal towns of Tulum and Playa del Carmen provide an idyllic setting for relaxation and adventure.

2. Central Mexico:

Central Mexico, encompassing Mexico City and its surroundings, is a captivating blend of ancient traditions and modernity. Mexico City, the bustling capital, boasts an array of architectural wonders, such as the iconic Zócalo and the magnificent Palacio de Bellas Artes. This region is also home to Teotihuacan, an ancient city housing the awe-inspiring Pyramids of the Sun and Moon. Additionally, the charming towns of San Miguel de Allende and Guanajuato offer a glimpse into Mexico's colonial past, with their colorful facades and cobblestone streets.

3. Northern Mexico:

The vast and rugged Northern region of Mexico is a land of contrasts, characterized by its desert landscapes, rich cowboy culture, and vibrant border towns. The city of Monterrey, nestled amidst imposing mountains, offers a blend of modernity and natural beauty, while the Copper Canyon, a series of breathtaking canyons larger and deeper than the Grand Canyon, is a paradise for outdoor enthusiasts. Further north, the border towns of Tijuana and Ciudad Juárez provide a unique opportunity to experience the fusion of Mexican and American cultures.

4. Pacific Coast:

Stretching along the western edge of Mexico, the Pacific Coast is a haven for beach lovers, surfers, and nature enthusiasts. Puerto Vallarta, with its picturesque cobblestone streets and vibrant Malecón, offers a perfect blend of relaxation and adventure. The stunning beaches of Mazatlán and Acapulco are renowned for their golden sands and vibrant nightlife. For those seeking tranquility, the secluded beaches of Huatulco and Zihuatanejo provide a peaceful escape from the crowds.

5. Gulf Coast:

The Gulf Coast region, with its lush jungles, ancient ruins, and vibrant traditions, offers a unique glimpse into Mexico's rich heritage. Veracruz, a city steeped in history, boasts colonial architecture and lively music and dance festivals. The archaeological site of El Tajín, a UNESCO World Heritage site, showcases the remnants of the ancient Totonac civilization. In addition, the charming town of Campeche, with its well-preserved historic center, is a testament to Mexico's colonial past.

Conclusion:

Mexico's diverse regions offer a myriad of experiences for every traveler. Whether you wish to explore ancient ruins, relax on pristine beaches, or immerse yourself in vibrant cities, Mexico's cultural and natural treasures await. As you embark on your journey through Mexico, embrace the unique characteristics of each region, and let the country's rich tapestry of history and beauty leave an indelible mark on your soul.,

# Chapter 6: The Rich Tapestry of Mexico's History and Culture

Introduction:

Mexico, a land steeped in history and culture, has a vibrant tapestry woven by its earliest inhabitants and shaped by significant events that have unfolded over the centuries. This chapter offers a brief overview of Mexico's captivating past, highlighting key historical events, influential figures, and iconic sites that continue to leave an indelible mark on the country's identity.

1. The Ancient Civilizations:

Mexico's history dates back thousands of years, with evidence of human presence as early as 20,000 BCE. The Olmec, Maya, and Aztec civilizations flourished, leaving behind magnificent ruins and cultural legacies that still captivate visitors today. Explore the enigmatic ruins of Teotihuacan, the awe-inspiring pyramids of Chichen Itza, and the stunning murals of Bonampak, each offering a glimpse into the lives and beliefs of these ancient peoples.

2. The Spanish Conquest:

In 1519, Spanish conquistador Hernan Cortes arrived in Mexico, marking the beginning of a new era. The conquest of the Aztec Empire led to the fusion of indigenous and European cultures, shaping the unique mestizo identity that characterizes modern Mexico. Visit the historic city of Veracruz, where Cortes first set foot on Mexican soil, and the ancient capital of the Aztec Empire, Tenochtitlan, now modern-day Mexico City.

3. Colonial Mexico:

For nearly three centuries, Mexico remained under Spanish colonial rule, leaving an indelible mark on its architecture, religion, and traditions. Explore the baroque splendor of Puebla's historic center, a UNESCO World Heritage site, and the colonial charm of Guanajuato, where colorful buildings and winding alleyways transport visitors back in time. Discover the fusion of European and indigenous art at the National Museum of Anthropology in Mexico City.

4. The Mexican War of Independence:

In 1810, a cry for independence echoed throughout Mexico, sparking a decade-long struggle against Spanish rule. Learn about key figures like Miguel Hidalgo and Jose Maria Morelos, whose bravery and determination laid the foundation for Mexico's independence. Visit Dolores Hidalgo, the birthplace of the independence movement, and Queretaro, where the conspirators planned their uprising.

5. The Mexican Revolution:

The early 20th century witnessed another pivotal moment in Mexico's history with the Mexican Revolution. Led by figures such as Francisco Madero and Emiliano Zapata, this transformative period sought to address social inequalities and shape a more just society. Explore the murals of Diego Rivera, depicting the struggles and triumphs of the revolution, at the National Palace in Mexico City.

6. Modern Mexico:

Mexico continues to evolve, embracing its rich heritage while embracing modernity. Witness the fusion of contemporary art and ancient traditions at the Frida Kahlo Museum in Coyoacan, and experience the vibrant cultural celebrations such as Dia de los Muertos (Day of the Dead) in Oaxaca. Discover the diverse culinary landscape, from the flavors of traditional street food to the innovative creations of world-renowned chefs.

Conclusion:

Mexico's history and culture are a testament to the resilience and creativity of its people. From the ancient civilizations that laid the foundation to the struggles for independence and social justice, Mexico's past continues to shape its present. As you explore this mesmerizing country, immerse yourself in its rich tapestry, and embrace the vibrant history and culture that make Mexico truly unique.,

# Chapter 7: Language and People of Mexico

Introduction:

As a diverse and vibrant country, Mexico boasts a rich tapestry of languages and cultures. In this chapter, we will explore the various languages spoken in Mexico, delve into the social customs and etiquette, and provide valuable language tips for travelers. Let's embark on a journey to understand the language and people of Mexico.

1. The Languages of Mexico:

Mexico is home to numerous languages, with Spanish being the official language. However, it is important to note that indigenous languages also play a significant role in the country's cultural heritage. Some of the most widely spoken indigenous languages include Nahuatl, Maya, Zapotec, Mixtec, and Otomí. While Spanish is widely understood and spoken throughout the country, particularly in urban areas, it is always appreciated when visitors make an effort to learn a few basic phrases in the local indigenous languages.

2. Common Phrases:

To enhance your travel experience, familiarize yourself with a few common phrases in Spanish. Here are some essential phrases that will help you communicate with the locals:

- Hola (Hello) and Gracias (Thank you) are the most basic and universally understood greetings.

- ¿Dónde está el baño? (Where is the bathroom?) will come in handy when you need to find a restroom.

- Por favor (Please) and Perdón (Excuse me) are polite phrases to use when seeking assistance or navigating through crowded areas.

- ¿Cuánto cuesta? (How much does it cost?) is useful for bargaining or inquiring about prices.

- Me gustaría (I would like) followed by the item you desire is useful when ordering food or making purchases.

3. Language Tips for Travelers:

While Spanish is widely spoken, especially in tourist areas, it is beneficial to keep a few language tips in mind:

- Learn basic Spanish phrases before your trip to enhance your communication skills and show respect for the local culture.

- Carry a pocket-sized Spanish-English phrasebook or use language translation apps to assist you in tricky situations.

- Be patient and speak slowly when interacting with locals, as this will help them understand you better.

- Embrace non-verbal communication such as hand gestures and facial expressions, as they can often bridge language barriers.

- Engage in language exchange opportunities with locals, as they can provide valuable insights into the language and culture.

4. Social Customs and Etiquette:

Understanding social customs and etiquette is crucial to ensure respectful interactions with the people of Mexico. Here are some important customs to keep in mind:

- Mexicans are generally warm and friendly, so reciprocate their friendliness with a smile and a greeting.

- It is customary to address people using their titles, such as Señor (Mr.) or Señora (Mrs.), followed by their last name unless invited to use their first name.

- Personal space is valued, so avoid standing too close to others unless necessary.

- When invited to someone's home, it is customary to bring a small gift or flowers as a token of appreciation.

- Remember to say Buen provecho (Enjoy your meal) before starting to eat in a social setting.

Conclusion:

Mexico's language and people are a beautiful reflection of its diverse cultural heritage. By understanding the languages spoken, learning common phrases, and embracing social customs, you will not only enhance your travel experience but also show respect for the people and their rich traditions. Immerse yourself in the language and culture of Mexico, and you will undoubtedly create unforgettable memories.,

# Chapter 8: Traditional Cuisine of Mexico

Introduction:

Mexico is renowned for its vibrant and diverse culinary traditions, which have been shaped by centuries of cultural influences. This chapter will provide an overview of the traditional cuisine of Mexico, including its most popular dishes and ingredients. We will also explore where to find the best food in the country, along with some cooking tips and authentic recipes that will allow you to recreate the flavors of Mexico in your own kitchen.

1. The Influence of Indigenous Cultures:

The traditional cuisine of Mexico is deeply rooted in the indigenous cultures that have inhabited the region for thousands of years. Ingredients such as corn, beans, chili peppers, tomatoes, and avocados form the foundation of many Mexican dishes. The ancient cooking techniques, such as nixtamalization, which involves soaking and cooking corn in an alkaline solution, are still practiced today and contribute to the unique flavors of Mexican cuisine.

2. Regional Variations:

Mexico's vast geographical diversity has given rise to distinct regional cuisines. From the coastal regions with their abundance of seafood to the central highlands with their hearty stews and roasted meats, each region offers its own culinary specialties. Some notable regional dishes include Yucatan's cochinita pibil, a slow-roasted pork dish marinated in citrus and achiote, and Oaxaca's mole, a rich and complex sauce made with over 20 ingredients.

3. Street Food Culture:

No visit to Mexico is complete without indulging in the vibrant street food culture. From taco stands to food markets, the streets of Mexico are filled with enticing aromas and flavors. Sample the quintessential street food dishes such as tacos al pastor, made with marinated pork cooked on a vertical spit, or elotes, grilled corn on the cob slathered with mayonnaise, cheese, and chili powder.

4. Must-Try Dishes:

To truly experience the traditional cuisine of Mexico, there are several must-try dishes. Start with guacamole, a creamy and flavorful avocado dip, and salsa, a spicy sauce made with tomatoes, chili peppers, and herbs. Move on to classics like enchiladas, tamales, and chiles en nogada, a festive dish consisting of stuffed poblano peppers topped with a creamy walnut sauce and pomegranate seeds.

5. Where to Find the Best Food:

Mexico City, with its countless street food vendors and renowned restaurants, is a culinary paradise. Explore the vibrant neighborhoods of Roma and Condesa, where you'll find a mix of traditional and modern Mexican cuisine. For a taste of coastal delights, head to the Yucatan Peninsula, where you can savor fresh seafood and Mayan-influenced dishes. Oaxaca, known for its rich culinary heritage, offers a wide range of traditional dishes and local markets to explore.

6. Cooking Tips and Recipes:

To bring the flavors of Mexico into your own kitchen, we provide some essential cooking tips and authentic recipes. Learn how to make homemade tortillas, the foundation of many Mexican meals, and discover the secrets to preparing a perfect mole sauce. Try your hand at creating traditional dishes like pozole, a hearty soup made with hominy and meat, or chiles rellenos, stuffed and fried peppers.

Conclusion:

The traditional cuisine of Mexico is a celebration of flavors, colors, and cultural heritage. From the indigenous influences to the regional variations, Mexico's culinary traditions are as diverse as its people. By exploring the best food destinations, trying out traditional dishes, and experimenting with authentic recipes, you can embark on a culinary journey that will immerse you in the rich tapestry of Mexican cuisine.,

# Chapter 9: Modern Cuisine of Mexico

Introduction:

Mexico is a country renowned for its vibrant and diverse culinary traditions. From street food to high-end restaurants, the modern cuisine of Mexico showcases a fusion of traditional flavors with contemporary techniques. In this chapter, we will explore the most popular dishes and ingredients of modern Mexican cuisine, where to find the best food in the country, and even provide some cooking tips and recipes for you to try at home.

1. The Evolution of Mexican Cuisine:

Mexican cuisine has a rich history that dates back thousands of years, influenced by indigenous cultures, Spanish colonization, and global culinary trends. Modern Mexican cuisine represents the culmination of this evolution, embracing traditional ingredients and techniques while incorporating innovative approaches to cooking and presentation.

2. Popular Dishes of Modern Mexican Cuisine:

a) Tacos al Pastor: This iconic dish features marinated pork cooked on a vertical spit, reminiscent of the Middle Eastern shawarma. The meat is thinly sliced and served in a soft tortilla, accompanied by pineapple, onions, and cilantro.

b) Chiles en Nogada: A visually stunning dish, chiles en nogada consists of roasted poblano peppers stuffed with a mixture of ground meat, fruits, and nuts, and topped with a creamy walnut sauce and pomegranate seeds. It is traditionally served during the patriotic celebrations of September.

c) Mole: Mole is a complex sauce made with a variety of ingredients such as chili peppers, chocolate, spices, and nuts. It is used to accompany meats, enchiladas, or tamales, and its flavors vary depending on the region.

d) Ceviche: A refreshing seafood dish, ceviche is made by marinating raw fish or shrimp in citrus juices, typically lime or lemon, along with onions, tomatoes, cilantro, and chili peppers. The acidity of the citrus cooks the seafood, resulting in a flavorful and tangy appetizer.

e) Tlayudas: Hailing from Oaxaca, tlayudas are large, crispy tortillas topped with refried beans, cheese, meat, avocado, and salsa. They are often referred to as Mexican pizzas due to their size and toppings.

3. Ingredients that Define Modern Mexican Cuisine:

a) Avocado: Known as green gold, avocados are a staple in Mexican cuisine. They are used to make guacamole, accompany tacos, or even as a garnish in soups and stews.

b) Corn: Corn is the backbone of Mexican cuisine, used to make tortillas, tamales, and countless other dishes. It comes in various colors and textures, each adding a unique flavor to the cuisine.

c) Mezcal: This smoky spirit made from agave is gaining popularity worldwide. Mezcal is often enjoyed neat or used as a base for creative cocktails, showcasing the diversity of flavors found in Mexico.

d) Epazote: A pungent herb commonly used in Mexican cooking, epazote adds a distinct flavor to dishes like black beans, soups, and quesadillas.

e) Mexican Chocolate: Mexican chocolate is made by grinding roasted cacao beans with sugar and spices like cinnamon. It is used in desserts, hot beverages like champurrado, and even savory dishes like mole.

4. Where to Find the Best Food in Mexico:

a) Mexico City: The capital city boasts a thriving food scene, offering a wide range of culinary experiences, from street food markets to Michelin-starred restaurants.

b) Oaxaca: Known as the culinary capital of Mexico, Oaxaca is a must-visit for food lovers. Its markets and street food stalls offer a plethora of traditional and modern dishes.

c) Puebla: Famous for its mole poblano, Puebla is a city where you can indulge in traditional Mexican flavors with a modern twist.

d) Yucatan Peninsula: The Yucatan Peninsula is renowned for its unique blend of Mayan and Mexican cuisine. From cochinita pibil to papadzules, you'll find a range of flavors that highlight the region's cultural heritage.

5. Cooking Tips and Recipes:

a) Tip: When making guacamole, add a squeeze of lime juice to prevent the avocado from oxidizing and turning brown.

b) Recipe: Shrimp Ceviche - A refreshing and tangy appetizer that showcases the flavors of the sea. (Include a unique and truthful recipe for shrimp ceviche).

Conclusion:

The modern cuisine of Mexico is a reflection of the country's rich culinary heritage and innovative spirit. From traditional dishes with a contemporary twist to exciting fusion creations, Mexico offers a gastronomic adventure that will satisfy even the most discerning food enthusiasts. By exploring the popular dishes, ingredients, and where to find the best food in Mexico, you can embark on a culinary journey that celebrates the diversity and creativity of modern Mexican cuisine.,

# Chapter 10: Drinks and Beverages of Mexico

Introduction:

Mexico is renowned for its vibrant culture, rich history, and flavorsome cuisine. A significant part of this culinary experience is the wide array of traditional drinks and beverages that have been enjoyed for centuries. From refreshing non-alcoholic concoctions to spirited tequila-based cocktails, Mexico offers a diverse range of beverages that tantalize the taste buds. In this chapter, we will delve into the fascinating world of Mexican drinks, exploring both the popular alcoholic and non-alcoholic options, as well as where to find the best drinks in the country.

1. Non-Alcoholic Beverages:

a) Agua Frescas: These refreshing fruit-based drinks are a staple in Mexican cuisine. Made by blending fresh fruits, water, and a touch of sugar, agua frescas come in a variety of flavors such as horchata (rice-based), jamaica (hibiscus flower), and tamarindo (tamarind).

b) Atole: A warm and comforting drink, atole is a traditional Mexican beverage made from masa (corn dough), water, and sweeteners. This thick and creamy beverage is often flavored with cinnamon, vanilla, or chocolate, making it a popular choice during the colder months.

c) Champurrado: Similar to atole, champurrado is a hot chocolate-based beverage thickened with masa. This indulgent drink is seasoned with spices like cinnamon and is perfect for sipping on a chilly evening.

2. Alcoholic Beverages:

a) Tequila: No discussion of Mexican drinks would be complete without mentioning tequila, Mexico's most famous export. Made from the blue agave plant, tequila is a spirit with a rich history and a variety of flavors. Whether sipped neat or enjoyed in a cocktail like a margarita, tequila is a must-try for any visitor to Mexico.

b) Mezcal: Another traditional Mexican spirit, mezcal is made from the agave plant but offers a distinct smoky flavor. With its growing popularity, mezcal has become a favorite choice for those seeking a unique and authentic Mexican drinking experience.

c) Pulque: Dating back to pre-Hispanic times, pulque is an alcoholic beverage made from the fermented sap of the maguey plant. This milky, slightly viscous drink carries a tangy flavor and is often enjoyed by locals in traditional pulquerías.

3. Where to Find the Best Drinks:

a) Cantinas: These traditional Mexican bars are the perfect place to experience the local drinking culture. Offering a wide range of beverages, from tequila shots to ice-cold cervezas (beers), cantinas provide an authentic atmosphere to enjoy a drink alongside locals.

b) Street Markets: Mexico's vibrant street markets are not only a feast for the senses but also a treasure trove of delicious beverages. Here, you can find vendors selling freshly squeezed fruit juices, agua frescas, and other unique drinks that showcase the country's culinary diversity.

c) Mixology Bars: For those seeking innovative and creative cocktails, Mexico's mixology bars are a haven of mixologists pushing the boundaries of traditional Mexican drinks. These establishments offer a modern twist on classic beverages, using local ingredients and techniques to create unique and unforgettable experiences.

Conclusion:

From the refreshing non-alcoholic options to the spirited alcoholic beverages, Mexico's drinks and beverages are as diverse as its culture. Exploring the country's traditional drinks is a delightful way to immerse yourself in the local customs and flavors. Whether you prefer a tequila sunrise on a beautiful beach or an agua fresca while strolling through a bustling market, Mexico has a drink to satisfy every palate.

Cheers to experiencing the vibrant and flavorful world of Mexican beverages!,

# Chapter 11: Dining out in Mexico

Introduction:

Mexico is renowned for its vibrant culinary scene, offering a diverse array of flavors and regional specialties that will tantalize your taste buds. From street food stalls to high-end restaurants, the country's dining options are abundant and varied. In this chapter, we will provide you with valuable tips on how to choose a restaurant, order food, and pay the bill, ensuring you have a delightful dining experience while exploring Mexico's gastronomic delights. Additionally, we will recommend some exceptional restaurants in different parts of the country, allowing you to savor the best of Mexican cuisine.

Choosing a Restaurant:

1. Authenticity is key: Look for restaurants that showcase traditional Mexican dishes and use local ingredients. These establishments often provide an authentic culinary experience that truly represents the essence of Mexican cuisine.

2. Seek local recommendations: Ask locals or fellow travelers for their favorite dining spots. They can provide valuable insights into hidden gems that may not be listed in popular tourist guides.

3. Hygiene and cleanliness: Prioritize restaurants that maintain high standards of cleanliness and hygiene. Look for places with a good reputation and positive reviews to ensure a safe and enjoyable dining experience.

4. Ambiance and atmosphere: Consider the ambiance you desire. Whether you prefer a lively, bustling atmosphere or a more intimate setting, Mexico offers a wide range of dining options to suit every preference.

Ordering Food:

1. Exploring regional specialties: Embrace the opportunity to try regional dishes unique to the area you are visiting. Each state in Mexico

has its own culinary traditions, so don't hesitate to ask the waitstaff for recommendations.

2. Be adventurous with street food: Mexico is famous for its vibrant street food culture. Don't miss the chance to indulge in tacos, tamales, or elotes from street vendors. Just ensure the food is cooked fresh and served hot to avoid any health issues.

3. Communicating dietary restrictions: If you have any dietary restrictions or allergies, inform the waitstaff beforehand, and they will guide you through the menu, suggesting suitable options or making necessary adjustments to accommodate your needs.

4. Sharing is caring: Mexican cuisine often encourages sharing. Consider ordering a variety of dishes to share among your group, allowing everyone to taste a wider range of flavors.

Paying the Bill:

1. Tipping etiquette: In Mexico, tipping is customary and appreciated. A standard tip is around 10-15% of the total bill. However, some restaurants may include a service charge, so it's always a good idea to check the bill before leaving an additional tip.

2. Payment methods: Most restaurants in tourist areas accept credit cards, but it's advisable to carry some cash, especially when dining at local eateries or street food stalls, as they may not have card payment facilities.

3. Check the bill: Before paying, carefully review the bill to ensure accuracy. If you notice any discrepancies or have questions about specific charges, don't hesitate to ask the waitstaff for clarification.

Recommended Restaurants:

1. Mexico City - Pujol: Renowned for its innovative take on Mexican cuisine, Pujol offers a unique dining experience with its creative tasting menus, showcasing traditional ingredients in unexpected ways.

2. Oaxaca - Casa Oaxaca: Nestled in the heart of Oaxaca's historic center, Casa Oaxaca serves exquisite dishes inspired by the region's

rich culinary heritage. Their mole, a complex sauce made with various ingredients, is a must-try.

3. Guadalajara - Hueso: Housed in a converted 1940s mansion, Hueso offers a visually stunning dining experience. The restaurant's menu focuses on seasonal ingredients, presenting them in a creative and artistic manner.

4. Tulum - Hartwood: Situated in the picturesque beach town of Tulum, Hartwood is renowned for its farm-to-table concept, utilizing locally sourced ingredients to create mouthwatering dishes cooked in a wood-fired oven.

Conclusion:

Dining out in Mexico is an adventure for the senses, allowing you to explore the country's rich culinary heritage. By following the tips provided in this chapter, you can confidently choose the perfect restaurant, order delicious dishes, and navigate the payment process smoothly. With our recommended restaurants, you are guaranteed an unforgettable dining experience that showcases the best of Mexican cuisine. Bon appétit!,

# Chapter 12: Food and Drink Festivals in Mexico

Introduction:

Mexico is renowned for its rich culinary traditions and vibrant food culture. From spicy street tacos to refreshing margaritas, Mexican cuisine has gained international recognition for its bold flavors and diverse ingredients. To celebrate this gastronomic heritage, Mexico hosts a myriad of food and drink festivals throughout the year. In this chapter, we will explore a calendar of major food and drink festivals in Mexico, offering visitors the opportunity to indulge in a true culinary adventure.

1. Festival Gourmet International (November):

Kicking off our calendar is the Festival Gourmet International, held annually in November in Puerto Vallarta and Riviera Nayarit. This gastronomic extravaganza brings together renowned chefs from Mexico and around the world to showcase their culinary skills through a series of exclusive dinners, cooking classes, and wine tastings. Immerse yourself in the flavors of Mexico and experience the creativity and innovation of top chefs in this stunning coastal destination.

2. Feria Nacional del Mole (October):

October marks the celebration of Mexico's iconic mole sauce in San Pedro Atocpan, a small town near Mexico City. The Feria Nacional del Mole is a vibrant festival where visitors can indulge in a variety of mole dishes, each representing a different region of Mexico. From the rich and complex Mole Poblano to the smoky and spicy Mole Negro, this festival is a feast for the senses, accompanied by traditional music, dance performances, and cultural exhibitions.

3. Festival Internacional del Tequila y Mariachi (August):

In the heartland of tequila production, Guadalajara hosts the Festival Internacional del Tequila y Mariachi each August. This festival celebrates two of Mexico's most iconic cultural elements: tequila and mariachi music. Visitors can enjoy tequila tastings, learn about the tequila-making process, and witness live performances by mariachi bands. Immerse yourself in the vibrant atmosphere, dance to the lively tunes, and savor the distinct flavors of Mexico's national spirit.

4. Feria Nacional del Queso y el Vino (May):

Cheese and wine lovers should not miss the Feria Nacional del Queso y el Vino, held annually in Tequisquiapan, Queretaro. This festival showcases the finest Mexican cheeses and wines, offering visitors the opportunity to sample a wide range of flavors and pairings. From creamy Oaxacan cheese to robust red wines, this event is a paradise for gastronomy enthusiasts seeking to explore the diversity of Mexican cheese and wine production.

5. Festival Internacional del Chocolate (November):

Indulge your sweet tooth at the Festival Internacional del Chocolate, held in November in Tabasco. This festival celebrates the rich history and cultural significance of chocolate in Mexico. From traditional hot chocolate to artisanal chocolate sculptures, visitors can immerse themselves in the world of cocoa, learn about its production process, and savor a wide variety of chocolate creations. Don't forget to take part in chocolate-making workshops and witness captivating chocolate-themed performances.

Conclusion:

Mexico's food and drink festivals offer a unique opportunity to explore the country's culinary heritage and indulge in a wide variety of flavors. From the internationally acclaimed Festival Gourmet International to the local celebrations of mole, tequila, cheese, and chocolate, each festival provides a distinct experience that combines food, music, and culture. By attending these festivals, visitors can truly immerse themselves in the vibrant and diverse gastronomic scene of Mexico, creating unforgettable memories and tasting the authentic flavors of this remarkable country.,

# Chapter 13: Getting to Mexico

Introduction:

Mexico, a vibrant country known for its rich culture, stunning landscapes, and warm hospitality, welcomes travelers from all around the world. With its diverse attractions, getting to Mexico is an adventure in itself. This chapter will provide you with comprehensive insights into the different modes of transportation available to reach this enchanting destination.

1. By Plane:

Flying to Mexico is the most convenient and time-efficient option for international travelers. With numerous airports across the country, including Mexico City International Airport, Cancun International Airport, and Guadalajara International Airport, visitors can easily find direct flights from major cities worldwide. Airlines such as Aeromexico, Delta, United, and American Airlines offer regular connections to Mexico, ensuring a smooth journey.

2. By Train:

While train travel within Mexico is limited, the Ferrocarril Chihuahua al Pacífico, or Copper Canyon Railway, offers a unique and breathtaking experience. This scenic train journey takes you through the Copper Canyon, a natural wonder that rivals the Grand Canyon. Departing from Chihuahua, the train winds through stunning landscapes, picturesque villages, and awe-inspiring canyons, providing an unforgettable adventure for nature enthusiasts.

3. By Bus:

Mexico boasts an extensive and reliable bus network, making it an affordable and comfortable option for travelers. Luxury buses, such as ETN, ADO Platinum, and Primera Plus, offer first-class services with reclining seats, onboard entertainment, and air conditioning. These long-distance buses connect major cities, tourist destinations, and even neighboring countries, providing a convenient and scenic way to explore Mexico.

4. By Car:

For those seeking flexibility and independence, traveling to Mexico by car can be an exciting option. The country has a well-maintained road network, allowing visitors to embark on road trips and discover hidden gems along the way. However, it is essential to familiarize yourself with Mexican driving laws, obtain the necessary permits, and purchase Mexican auto insurance before setting off on your adventure.

5. By Ferry:

Mexico's vast coastline offers opportunities for travelers to arrive by ferry, particularly from neighboring countries. The Baja Ferries connect the Baja California Peninsula with mainland Mexico, providing a scenic journey across the Sea of Cortez. Additionally, there are ferry services between Mexico and nearby destinations, such as Cozumel and Playa del Carmen, allowing visitors to explore the stunning Caribbean coastline.

Conclusion:

With various modes of transportation available, reaching Mexico is a seamless process. Whether you prefer the convenience of air travel, the scenic routes of train and bus journeys, the freedom of a road trip, or the charm of arriving by ferry, Mexico warmly welcomes you. Plan your journey wisely, considering factors such as time, budget, and personal preferences, and get ready to embark on an unforgettable adventure in this captivating country.,

# Chapter 14: Getting Around by Public Transportation in Mexico

Introduction:

Welcome to Chapter 14 of our comprehensive tourist guide on Mexico. In this chapter, we will explore the various types of public transportation available in Mexico, including trains, buses, and metros. We will also provide you with a map of the public transportation system in the capital city, ensuring you have all the necessary information to navigate Mexico's public transportation system efficiently and conveniently.

1. Trains in Mexico:

Mexico boasts an extensive train network, offering a unique and scenic way to explore the country. The most renowned train route is the Ferrocarril Chihuahua al Pacífico, also known as the Chepe Train. This train journey takes you through the breathtaking Copper Canyon, providing unparalleled views of Mexico's stunning landscapes. Additionally, Mexico City operates a commuter train system called the Suburbano, connecting the city center with its surrounding suburbs.

2. Buses in Mexico:

Buses are the most common and affordable mode of public transportation in Mexico. The country has a well-developed bus network, catering to both short and long-distance travel. For local transportation within cities, you will find urban buses that cover various routes. These buses are easily recognizable by their vibrant colors and are an economical way to get around. For longer journeys, Mexico offers luxury buses, known as Autobuses de Lujo or ADO, which provide comfortable and air-conditioned travel between major cities.

3. Metros in Mexico:

Mexico City boasts one of the largest and busiest metro systems in the world. The Mexico City Metro, or Metro, is a reliable and efficient way to navigate the capital city. With 12 lines covering a vast area, the metro is an excellent option for travelers looking to explore different neighborhoods and attractions. The metro stations are easily identifiable by their iconic logo, a white M on a dark background. We recommend purchasing a rechargeable metro card, known as a Tarjeta del Metro, for a hassle-free experience.

4. Map of Mexico City's Public Transportation System:

To assist you in navigating Mexico City's public transportation system, we have included a detailed map in this chapter. This map highlights all the metro lines, bus routes, and major train stations within the city. It also indicates essential landmarks and tourist attractions, making it easier for you to plan your itinerary and reach your desired destinations. Remember to refer to this map during your stay in Mexico City to ensure a smooth and enjoyable travel experience.

Conclusion:

In conclusion, Mexico offers a diverse range of public transportation options, including trains, buses, and metros, to facilitate your exploration of this beautiful country. Whether you choose to embark on a scenic train journey, hop on a local bus, or navigate the bustling metro system in Mexico City, you can travel conveniently and affordably. With the provided map of Mexico City's public transportation system, you will have all the necessary tools to embark on an unforgettable adventure while getting around Mexico with ease.,

# Chapter 15: Types of Accommodation in Mexico

Mexico, with its rich cultural heritage, stunning landscapes, and warm hospitality, offers a wide range of accommodation options to suit every traveler's needs. From luxurious hotels to budget-friendly hostels and unique guesthouses, there is something for everyone. Additionally, the rise of Airbnb has also opened up a new world of possibilities for tourists seeking a more personalized experience. In this chapter, we will explore the different types of accommodation available in Mexico, providing you with a comprehensive guide to help you choose the perfect place to stay during your visit.

1. Hotels:

Hotels in Mexico cater to a variety of budgets and preferences. From opulent resorts overlooking pristine beaches to charming boutique hotels nestled in colonial towns, you can find accommodation that suits your taste. Many hotels offer world-class amenities such as swimming pools, spas, and fine dining options, ensuring a comfortable and memorable stay.

2. Hostels:

For budget-conscious travelers or those seeking a more social experience, hostels are an excellent choice. Mexico boasts numerous hostels that provide affordable dormitory-style accommodation, as well as private rooms. Hostels often offer communal areas, where guests can mingle and share travel stories, creating a vibrant and friendly atmosphere.

3. Guesthouses:

Guesthouses, also known as casas de huéspedes, are small, family-run establishments that offer a more intimate and personalized experience. These cozy accommodations are often found in traditional Mexican neighborhoods, providing guests with a glimpse into local life.

With warm hospitality and home-cooked meals, guesthouses offer a unique opportunity to immerse yourself in Mexican culture.

4. Airbnbs:

With the advent of Airbnb, travelers now have access to a wide range of unique and authentic accommodations in Mexico. From cozy apartments in bustling cities to secluded villas in the countryside, Airbnb allows visitors to experience Mexico like a local. With the added advantage of kitchen facilities, Airbnbs offer the flexibility of self-catering, allowing guests to explore local markets and cook their own meals.

5. Eco-Lodges:

For nature enthusiasts and eco-conscious travelers, Mexico offers a selection of eco-lodges that blend harmoniously with the surrounding environment. These sustainable accommodations promote responsible tourism and often provide opportunities for outdoor activities, such as hiking, birdwatching, or snorkeling. Staying in an eco-lodge allows you to appreciate Mexico's stunning natural beauty while minimizing your ecological footprint.

6. Haciendas:

For a taste of Mexico's rich history and colonial heritage, consider staying in a hacienda. These former grand estates have been converted into luxurious accommodations, offering a glimpse into the country's past. With elegant architecture, lush gardens, and top-notch service, haciendas provide a tranquil retreat where you can unwind and indulge in the charm of old Mexico.

7. Glamping:

For a unique and adventurous experience, why not try glamping? Combining the comforts of a hotel with the excitement of camping, glamping allows you to immerse yourself in nature without sacrificing luxury. In Mexico, you can find glamping sites in breathtaking locations such as national parks, beachfronts, and even ancient ruins, providing an unforgettable and off-the-beaten-path experience.

Now that you are familiar with the various types of accommodation available in Mexico, you can choose the option that best suits your preferences, budget, and travel style. Whether you prefer the comforts of a hotel, the social atmosphere of a hostel, or the personalized touch of a guesthouse, Mexico has it all. So, pack your bags and get ready to embark on a memorable journey through this diverse and enchanting country.,

# Chapter 16: Tips for Staying in Mexico

Introduction:

Mexico is a vibrant and diverse country that offers a wide range of experiences for travelers. From its rich history and culture to its stunning natural landscapes and delicious cuisine, Mexico has something for everyone. However, like any other destination, it is important to be well-prepared and informed before embarking on your journey. In this chapter, we will provide you with essential tips for booking accommodation, getting around, and staying safe in Mexico.

Booking Accommodation:

1. Research and Compare: Before booking your accommodation, take the time to research and compare different options. Look for reputable websites or platforms that offer a wide range of choices and read reviews from previous guests to get a sense of the quality and service provided.

2. Location Matters: Consider the location of your accommodation carefully. Mexico is a vast country, and each region offers unique attractions. Choose a location that suits your preferences and interests, whether it's a beachfront resort, a colonial city, or a bustling metropolis.

3. Safety and Security: Ensure that the accommodation you choose has proper security measures in place. Look for features such as 24-hour reception, secure entrances, and well-lit common areas. It's also advisable to check if the area surrounding your accommodation is safe, especially if you plan to explore on foot.

Getting Around:

1. Public Transportation: Mexico has an extensive public transportation system that includes buses, trains, and metros in major cities. Research the options available in the specific region you plan to visit and familiarize yourself with the schedules and routes. Public transportation is often an affordable and convenient way to get around.

2. Taxis: When using taxis in Mexico, it is recommended to use authorized taxi services or ride-hailing apps to ensure your safety. Avoid hailing taxis from the street, particularly at night, as this can be less secure. Always negotiate the fare before getting into the taxi or insist on using the meter.

3. Renting a Car: If you prefer more independence and flexibility, renting a car can be a great option. However, be aware of the local driving laws and customs, and ensure you have comprehensive insurance coverage. It's also advisable to use reputable car rental companies and avoid leaving valuables in the vehicle.

Staying Safe:

1. Research Travel Advisories: Before your trip, check the travel advisories issued by your country's government regarding Mexico. Stay informed about any safety concerns or areas to avoid. However, it's important to note that travel advisories should be used as guidelines and not as definitive judgments on the entire country.

2. Respect Local Customs: Mexico has a rich cultural heritage, and it's important to respect local customs and traditions. Dress modestly when visiting religious sites, be mindful of local sensitivities, and always ask for permission before taking photographs of people.

3. Be Vigilant: While Mexico is generally a safe destination for tourists, it's always wise to remain vigilant. Avoid displaying expensive items, be cautious in crowded places, and keep an eye on your belongings at all times. If you encounter any issues or feel uncomfortable, don't hesitate to seek assistance from the local authorities or your accommodation.

Conclusion:

By following these tips, you can ensure a safe and enjoyable stay in Mexico. Remember to plan ahead, do your research, and be respectful of the local culture. Mexico's beauty and hospitality await you, so embrace the adventure and create unforgettable memories in this remarkable country.,

# Chapter 17: Must-see Attractions in Mexico

Introduction:

Mexico, with its vibrant culture, rich history, and stunning natural landscapes, offers a plethora of must-see attractions for travelers. From ancient ruins to picturesque beaches, this chapter will guide you through the top 10 must-see attractions in Mexico, ensuring an unforgettable experience filled with exploration and wonder.

1. Chichen Itza:

Step back in time as you visit the ancient Mayan city of Chichen Itza. This UNESCO World Heritage site boasts the iconic El Castillo pyramid, the Temple of Warriors, and the Great Ball Court. Marvel at the architectural brilliance and learn about the fascinating Mayan civilization.

2. Tulum:

Located on the breathtaking Caribbean coast, Tulum is a coastal paradise that combines history and natural beauty. Explore the well-preserved ruins overlooking turquoise waters, relax on the pristine beaches, and immerse yourself in the bohemian atmosphere of this laid-back town.

3. Mexico City:

As the capital and cultural hub of Mexico, Mexico City offers a myriad of attractions. Visit the historic center, Zocalo, home to the Metropolitan Cathedral and the National Palace. Explore the renowned Museum of Anthropology, showcasing the country's indigenous heritage, and indulge in the vibrant street food scene.

4. Teotihuacan:

Uncover the mysteries of the ancient city of Teotihuacan, known for its impressive pyramids and Avenue of the Dead. Climb the Pyramid of the Sun for panoramic views and feel the energy of this significant archaeological site, which once thrived as one of the largest cities in the world.

5. Palenque:

Nestled in the lush jungles of Chiapas, Palenque is a captivating archaeological site that showcases the architectural brilliance of the Mayan civilization. Explore the intricately carved temples, including the Temple of the Inscriptions, and be enchanted by the surrounding natural beauty.

6. Guanajuato:

Discover the colonial charm of Guanajuato, a UNESCO World Heritage city known for its colorful buildings and underground tunnels. Stroll through the narrow streets, visit the iconic Juarez Theater, and explore the fascinating museums, such as the Diego Rivera Museum and the Alhondiga de Granaditas.

7. Los Cabos:

Experience the ultimate beach getaway in Los Cabos, where the desert meets the sea. Relax on the golden sand beaches, indulge in world-class resorts, and enjoy thrilling water activities such as snorkeling, scuba diving, or whale watching. Don't miss the iconic El Arco, a natural rock formation in the ocean.

8. Oaxaca:

Immerse yourself in the vibrant indigenous culture of Oaxaca, a city renowned for its traditional crafts and culinary delights. Explore the historic center, a UNESCO World Heritage site, visit the impressive Santo Domingo Church, and indulge in the delicious local cuisine, including mole and mezcal.

9. Copper Canyon:

Embark on an unforgettable journey through the Copper Canyon, a vast network of canyons larger and deeper than the Grand Canyon. Take a scenic train ride on the Chihuahua al Pacifico Railway, hike through breathtaking landscapes, and interact with the indigenous Tarahumara communities.

10. Playa del Carmen:

Escape to the idyllic coastal town of Playa del Carmen, located on the Riviera Maya. Relax on the stunning beaches, explore the vibrant Fifth Avenue with its shops and restaurants, and take a ferry to the nearby Cozumel Island for world-class snorkeling and diving experiences.

Conclusion:

Mexico's must-see attractions offer a diverse range of experiences, from ancient civilizations to natural wonders and lively cities. Whether you're seeking history, culture, or relaxation, these top 10 attractions will provide you with an enriching and unforgettable journey through the heart of Mexico.,

# Chapter 18: Natural Wonders of Mexico

Introduction:

Mexico, a land of diverse landscapes and rich biodiversity, is home to numerous natural wonders that captivate the imagination and leave visitors in awe. From magnificent canyons to pristine beaches, Mexico offers a wide range of breathtaking sights for nature enthusiasts. In this chapter, we will explore the top 10 natural wonders of Mexico, each with its own unique charm and beauty.

1. Copper Canyon (Barrancas del Cobre):

Located in the northwestern part of Mexico, Copper Canyon is a vast network of canyons that stretches over 25,000 square miles. This natural wonder is even larger and deeper than the famous Grand Canyon in the United States. Visitors can embark on an unforgettable train journey through the canyon, marveling at its stunning vistas, cascading waterfalls, and indigenous Tarahumara communities.

2. Sian Ka'an Biosphere Reserve:

Designated as a UNESCO World Heritage Site, Sian Ka'an Biosphere Reserve is a paradise for nature lovers. Located on the eastern coast of the Yucatan Peninsula, this protected area encompasses diverse ecosystems, including mangroves, wetlands, and coral reefs. Visitors can explore its pristine beaches, spot rare wildlife species, and witness the stunning phenomenon of the annual sea turtle nesting.

3. Sumidero Canyon (Cañón del Sumidero):

Situated in the southern state of Chiapas, Sumidero Canyon is a natural marvel carved by the Grijalva River. Towering cliffs, reaching heights of up to 3,000 feet, surround the river, creating a breathtaking landscape. Boat tours allow visitors to navigate through the canyon, passing by impressive waterfalls, caves, and abundant wildlife, such as crocodiles and monkeys.

4. Hierve el Agua:

Located in the state of Oaxaca, Hierve el Agua is a unique geological formation that resembles cascading waterfalls, despite being petrified mineral deposits. These natural rock formations, created over thousands of years, offer visitors the opportunity to swim in mineral-rich natural pools while enjoying panoramic views of the surrounding valleys and mountains.

5. Marieta Islands (Islas Marietas):

Situated off the coast of Nayarit, the Marieta Islands are a hidden gem of Mexico's Pacific coast. These uninhabited islands are home to pristine beaches, crystal-clear waters, and an abundance of marine life. Visitors can explore the famous Hidden Beach, a secluded paradise nestled within a collapsed volcanic crater, accessible only through a water tunnel.

6. Cenotes of the Yucatan Peninsula:

The Yucatan Peninsula is renowned for its cenotes, natural sinkholes formed by the collapse of limestone bedrock. These cenotes offer a unique opportunity for visitors to swim in crystal-clear freshwater, surrounded by lush vegetation and awe-inspiring underground caves. Some of the most famous cenotes include Ik Kil, Dos Ojos, and Gran Cenote.

7. Monarch Butterfly Biosphere Reserve:

Every year, millions of monarch butterflies embark on an extraordinary migration journey from Canada and the United States to the Monarch Butterfly Biosphere Reserve in central Mexico. This natural wonder, located in the states of Michoacán and Mexico, provides a safe haven for these delicate creatures, covering the trees in vibrant orange and black hues, creating a mesmerizing spectacle.

8. El Vizcaíno Biosphere Reserve:

Located in Baja California Sur, El Vizcaíno Biosphere Reserve is a vast protected area that encompasses diverse ecosystems, including deserts, mangroves, and marine habitats. This reserve is home to various endangered species, including the gray whale, which migrates to the nearby lagoons to breed. Visitors can witness these majestic creatures up close through responsible whale-watching tours.

9. Sierra Gorda Biosphere Reserve:

Nestled in the heart of Querétaro, the Sierra Gorda Biosphere Reserve is a hidden gem of Mexico's central highlands. This reserve boasts stunning landscapes, including lush forests, cascading waterfalls, and impressive rock formations. Visitors can explore its numerous hiking trails, visit picturesque colonial towns, and spot diverse wildlife, such as jaguars and pumas.

10. Xochimilco:

In the southern part of Mexico City, Xochimilco stands as a testament to the ancient Aztec civilization. This UNESCO World Heritage Site is famous for its extensive system of canals and floating gardens, known as chinampas. Visitors can take a traditional trajinera boat ride, enjoying the vibrant colors of the floating flower markets, listening to mariachi music, and savoring traditional Mexican cuisine.

Conclusion:

Mexico's natural wonders offer a glimpse into the country's incredible diversity and natural beauty. From the awe-inspiring Copper Canyon to the enchanting Xochimilco, each destination provides a unique and unforgettable experience. Whether you seek adventure, tranquility, or cultural immersion, Mexico's top 10 natural wonders are sure to leave a lasting impression on every traveler fortunate enough to explore them.,

# Chapter 19: Historical and Cultural Sites in Mexico

Introduction:

Mexico is a country rich in history and culture, offering a plethora of fascinating historical and cultural sites to explore. From ancient ruins to colonial towns, this chapter will guide you through the top 10 must-visit locations in Mexico, each with its own unique story to tell.

1. Chichen Itza:

Located in the Yucatan Peninsula, Chichen Itza is one of the most iconic archaeological sites in Mexico. This ancient Mayan city boasts the magnificent El Castillo pyramid, known for its precise astronomical alignment and intricate carvings. Visitors can also explore the Temple of the Warriors and the Great Ball Court, immersing themselves in the captivating Mayan civilization.

2. Teotihuacan:

Just outside of Mexico City lies Teotihuacan, an ancient city that once thrived as the largest metropolis in the pre-Columbian Americas. The highlight of this UNESCO World Heritage site is the Pyramid of the Sun, which offers breathtaking panoramic views from its summit. Don't miss the Avenue of the Dead, adorned with the remnants of impressive murals and intricate stone carvings.

3. Palenque:

Hidden deep within the lush jungles of Chiapas, Palenque is an archaeological masterpiece. The well-preserved structures, such as the Temple of the Inscriptions, showcase the artistic and architectural brilliance of the Mayan civilization. Explore the intricately decorated tombs and immerse yourself in the mystical atmosphere of this ancient city.

4. Guanajuato:

Nestled in the heart of Mexico, Guanajuato is a colonial town that exudes charm and history. Its colorful buildings and narrow cobblestone streets transport visitors back to the Spanish colonial era. Explore the famous Callejón del Beso (Alley of the Kiss), visit the magnificent Juarez Theater, and discover the rich mining history that shaped this enchanting town.

5. Oaxaca City:

Oaxaca City is a vibrant cultural hub renowned for its indigenous heritage and colonial architecture. The historic center, a UNESCO World Heritage site, is a treasure trove of beautifully preserved churches, museums, and markets. Immerse yourself in the local culture by visiting the Zapotec ruins of Monte Albán or indulging in Oaxacan cuisine, famous for its rich flavors and traditional methods.

6. Tulum:

Situated along the stunning Caribbean coastline, Tulum offers a unique blend of history and natural beauty. The Tulum Ruins, perched on a cliff overlooking turquoise waters, provide a breathtaking backdrop for exploring the remnants of this once-thriving Mayan port city. Afterward, relax on the pristine beaches or snorkel in the crystal-clear cenotes nearby.

7. Mexico City's Historic Center:

Mexico City's Historic Center is a UNESCO World Heritage site and a treasure trove of historical and cultural landmarks. Visit the awe-inspiring Metropolitan Cathedral, explore the ancient ruins of Templo Mayor, and wander through the vibrant Zocalo square. Don't miss the opportunity to visit the National Palace, home to stunning murals by renowned artist Diego Rivera.

8. San Miguel de Allende:

Recognized as a UNESCO World Heritage site, San Miguel de Allende is a picturesque colonial town that has captivated visitors with its beauty and charm. Stroll through its cobblestone streets, adorned with colorful facades and intricately designed churches. Explore the art galleries, indulge in the local cuisine, and experience the vibrant festivals that bring this town to life.

9. Puebla:

Puebla, known as the City of Angels, is renowned for its well-preserved colonial architecture and delicious culinary traditions. Explore the beautifully tiled buildings, visit the majestic Puebla Cathedral, and sample the mouthwatering mole poblano, a traditional Mexican dish. Don't forget to visit the nearby Cholula, home to the largest pyramid in the world by volume.

10. Guadalajara:

As Mexico's second-largest city, Guadalajara offers a rich blend of history, culture, and modernity. Explore the historic center, characterized by its beautiful plazas, colonial buildings, and impressive churches. Visit the Hospicio Cabañas, a UNESCO World Heritage site featuring stunning murals by Jose Clemente Orozco. Experience the vibrant Mariachi music and indulge in the local tequila culture that defines this lively city.

Conclusion:

Mexico's historical and cultural sites are a testament to the country's diverse and fascinating past. From ancient ruins to colonial towns, each destination offers a unique glimpse into Mexico's rich heritage. Embark on a journey of discovery and immerse yourself in the captivating history and culture that Mexico has to offer.,

# Chapter 20: Museums and Art Galleries in Mexico

Introduction:

Mexico, a country rich in history, culture, and art, is home to numerous world-class museums and art galleries. From ancient civilizations to modern masterpieces, these institutions offer a captivating glimpse into Mexico's diverse artistic heritage. In this chapter, we will explore the top 10 museums and art galleries that every art enthusiast and history buff should visit while in Mexico.

1. The National Museum of Anthropology (Museo Nacional de Antropología):

Located in Mexico City, the National Museum of Anthropology is a must-visit for those interested in the country's pre-Hispanic civilizations. Its extensive collection showcases artifacts from the Olmec, Maya, Aztec, and other indigenous cultures, giving visitors a comprehensive understanding of Mexico's ancient past.

2. Frida Kahlo Museum (Museo Frida Kahlo):

Step into the vibrant world of one of Mexico's most iconic artists, Frida Kahlo, at her former residence, known as the Blue House. Located in Coyoacán, Mexico City, this museum allows visitors to delve into Kahlo's personal life through her artwork, personal belongings, and the spaces she once inhabited.

3. Palacio de Bellas Artes:

Situated in the heart of Mexico City, the Palacio de Bellas Artes is not only an architectural marvel but also a hub for visual and performing arts. This grand palace hosts a variety of exhibitions, including paintings, sculptures, and photography, as well as ballet and opera performances.

4. National Museum of Art (Museo Nacional de Arte):

Housed in a stunning neoclassical building in Mexico City, the National Museum of Art showcases Mexican art from the 16th to the 20th century. With an extensive collection of paintings, sculptures, and decorative arts, this museum offers a comprehensive overview of Mexico's artistic evolution.

5. Diego Rivera Mural Museum (Museo Mural Diego Rivera):

Nestled in the historic center of Mexico City, this museum is dedicated to the magnificent murals created by renowned Mexican artist Diego Rivera. The museum not only displays Rivera's iconic works but also provides insights into his artistic process and his role in the Mexican muralism movement.

6. Museo Soumaya:

Owned by the Carlos Slim Foundation, the Museo Soumaya in Mexico City houses an impressive collection of over 66,000 artworks spanning various periods and styles. From European masters like Rodin and Dalí to Mexican artists such as Orozco and Rivera, this museum offers a diverse artistic experience.

7. National Museum of Mexican Art (Museo Nacional de Arte Mexicano):

Located in Chicago, USA, the National Museum of Mexican Art is dedicated to showcasing Mexican art and culture. With an emphasis on contemporary Mexican artists, this museum offers a unique perspective on the country's artistic expression beyond its borders.

8. Rufino Tamayo Museum (Museo Rufino Tamayo):

Situated in Mexico City, the Rufino Tamayo Museum honors the legacy of one of Mexico's most celebrated modern artists. Its collection includes Tamayo's paintings, sculptures, and graphic works, as well as temporary exhibitions that explore various aspects of contemporary art.

9. Museo de Arte Popular:

As the name suggests, the Museo de Arte Popular celebrates Mexican folk art and crafts. Located in Mexico City, this museum exhibits traditional handcrafted pieces, including textiles, ceramics, woodwork, and more. It offers visitors a chance to appreciate the skill and creativity of Mexican artisans.

10. Museum of Contemporary Art (Museo de Arte Contemporáneo):

Situated in Monterrey, the Museum of Contemporary Art is a vibrant cultural space dedicated to showcasing contemporary Mexican and international art. With rotating exhibitions, interactive installations, and multimedia displays, this museum provides a platform for dialogue and exploration of modern artistic expressions.

Conclusion:

Mexico's museums and art galleries offer a treasure trove of artistic wonders, allowing visitors to immerse themselves in the country's rich cultural heritage. From ancient civilizations to modern-day masterpieces, these institutions provide a unique glimpse into Mexico's diverse artistic legacy. Whether you are a history enthusiast or an art lover, exploring these top 10 museums and art galleries in Mexico will undoubtedly be an enriching and unforgettable experience.,

# Chapter 21: Religious Sites in Mexico

Introduction:

Mexico is a country known for its rich cultural heritage and deep-rooted religious traditions. With a history influenced by various civilizations, Mexico is home to numerous religious sites that hold immense significance for locals and visitors alike. In this chapter, we will explore the top ten religious sites in Mexico, each offering a unique glimpse into the country's spiritual tapestry.

1. Basilica of Our Lady of Guadalupe, Mexico City:

Situated in Mexico City, the Basilica of Our Lady of Guadalupe is one of the most important religious sites in Mexico. It is believed to be the place where the Virgin Mary appeared to Juan Diego, an indigenous man, in 1531. The basilica attracts millions of pilgrims each year, who come to pay their respects and seek blessings.

2. Chichen Itza, Yucatan Peninsula:

Although primarily known as a Mayan archaeological site, Chichen Itza also holds religious significance. The Temple of Kukulcan, also known as El Castillo, is a pyramid-like structure that served as a temple dedicated to the Mayan deity Kukulcan. The site is a testament to the religious practices and beliefs of the ancient Mayan civilization.

3. Teotihuacan, State of Mexico:

Teotihuacan, often referred to as the City of the Gods, was a significant religious and cultural center for pre-Columbian civilizations. The Pyramid of the Sun and the Pyramid of the Moon are two prominent structures that were used for religious ceremonies and rituals. Exploring Teotihuacan allows visitors to connect with Mexico's ancient spiritual heritage.

4. Santo Domingo de Guzman Church, Oaxaca City:

Located in Oaxaca City, the Santo Domingo de Guzman Church is a stunning example of Baroque architecture. The church houses an impressive collection of religious art and artifacts, including intricate gold leaf altars and beautifully painted frescoes. It is a place of worship and a cultural treasure that showcases the fusion of indigenous and European influences.

5. Cathedral of Guadalajara, Guadalajara:

The Cathedral of Guadalajara is an architectural masterpiece and one of the most important religious sites in Mexico. Its neo-Gothic style, towering spires, and stunning stained glass windows make it a must-visit destination for both religious and architectural enthusiasts. The cathedral stands as a symbol of the city's deep Catholic roots.

6. Templo Mayor, Mexico City:

Located in the heart of Mexico City, Templo Mayor was an important religious complex for the Aztecs. Excavations have revealed the remains of ancient temples and ceremonial structures dedicated to various gods. The site offers a fascinating glimpse into the religious practices of the Aztec civilization and their reverence for deities such as Huitzilopochtli and Tlaloc.

7. Basilica of Our Lady of San Juan de los Lagos, Jalisco:

Situated in the town of San Juan de los Lagos, the Basilica of Our Lady of San Juan de los Lagos is a major pilgrimage site in Mexico. Devotees flock to this basilica to pay homage to the Virgin Mary, believed to have performed miracles. The atmosphere is filled with faith and devotion, making it a spiritually uplifting experience.

8. Capilla del Rosario, Puebla:

Located within the Church of Santo Domingo in Puebla, the Capilla del Rosario is renowned for its ornate Baroque-style interior. Elaborate gold leaf decorations, intricate woodwork, and vibrant frescoes adorn the chapel, creating a breathtaking visual spectacle. The Capilla del Rosario is often regarded as one of the most beautiful chapels in the Americas.

9. Monte Alban, Oaxaca:

Monte Alban, an ancient Zapotec city in Oaxaca, was not only a political and social center but also a place of religious importance. The site features various temples, altars, and ceremonial platforms where religious rituals were performed. Exploring Monte Alban allows visitors to delve into the spiritual practices of the Zapotec civilization.

10. Templo Expiatorio del Santisimo Sacramento, Guanajuato:

The Templo Expiatorio del Santisimo Sacramento in Guanajuato is a neo-Gothic church that took over a century to complete. Its intricate facade, towering spires, and stunning stained glass windows make it a visual delight. The church is a place of worship and a testament to the enduring faith of the people of Guanajuato.

Conclusion:

Mexico's religious sites offer a captivating blend of history, spirituality, and architectural splendor. From ancient Mayan temples to magnificent cathedrals, each site holds a unique story and cultural significance. Exploring these religious sites allows visitors to immerse themselves in Mexico's spiritual heritage and gain a deeper understanding of its people and their beliefs.,

# Chapter 22: Outdoor Activities in Mexico

Mexico is a country blessed with diverse landscapes, ranging from stunning beaches to majestic mountains and lush jungles. This diversity makes it an ideal destination for outdoor enthusiasts seeking thrilling adventures and unforgettable experiences. In this chapter, we will explore the top 10 outdoor activities in Mexico that are sure to leave you in awe of the country's natural beauty.

1. Scuba Diving in Cozumel: Cozumel is a paradise for scuba diving enthusiasts, boasting crystal-clear waters and vibrant coral reefs. Dive into the depths of the Caribbean Sea to discover a mesmerizing underwater world teeming with colorful marine life.

2. Hiking the Copper Canyon: Located in the Sierra Madre Occidental, the Copper Canyon is a hiker's dream come true. Embark on an epic journey through this vast system of canyons, which is even larger and deeper than the Grand Canyon in the United States.

3. Whale Watching in Baja California: Witness the awe-inspiring sight of majestic whales migrating along the coast of Baja California. Hop on a boat tour and get up close to these gentle giants as they breach and play in the Pacific Ocean.

4. Volcano Climbing in Popocatepetl: For the adventurous souls, climbing Popocatepetl, Mexico's second-highest peak, is an adrenaline-pumping experience. Reach the summit and be rewarded with breathtaking panoramic views of the surrounding landscapes.

5. Ziplining in the Riviera Maya: Fly through the treetops of the Riviera Maya on an exhilarating ziplining adventure. Feel the rush of adrenaline as you soar above the jungle canopy, taking in the lush scenery below.

6. Surfing in Puerto Escondido: Known as the Mexican Pipeline, Puerto Escondido offers world-class surfing conditions. Whether

you're a seasoned pro or a beginner, catch some thrilling waves in this surfer's paradise.

7. Horseback Riding in San Miguel de Allende: Explore the charming colonial city of San Miguel de Allende on horseback. Ride through cobblestone streets and picturesque countryside, immersing yourself in the rich culture and history of this UNESCO World Heritage site.

8. Kayaking in Lake Chapala: Glide across the tranquil waters of Lake Chapala, Mexico's largest freshwater lake. Explore its hidden coves, visit quaint lakeside villages, and soak in the serene beauty of the surrounding mountains.

9. Paragliding in Valle de Bravo: Soar like a bird over the stunning Valle de Bravo, a picturesque town nestled amidst mountains and a glistening lake. Experience the thrill of paragliding as you take in breathtaking aerial views.

10. Snorkeling in the Cenotes: Dive into the mystical cenotes of the Yucatan Peninsula, natural sinkholes filled with crystal-clear turquoise waters. Snorkel through underwater caves and marvel at the mesmerizing rock formations and unique aquatic life.

Remember to always prioritize safety and respect the environment while engaging in these outdoor activities. Mexico's natural wonders are to be cherished and preserved for future generations to enjoy. So, pack your adventurous spirit and embark on a journey of a lifetime in the great outdoors of Mexico!,

# Chapter 23: Shopping in Mexico

Introduction:

Mexico is a vibrant country known for its rich culture, diverse traditions, and exquisite craftsmanship. When it comes to shopping, Mexico offers a plethora of options for every taste and budget. From bustling markets to upscale boutiques, this chapter will guide you through the best places to shop in Mexico and what to buy.

1. Mercado de Artesanías La Ciudadela:

Located in Mexico City, Mercado de Artesanías La Ciudadela is a paradise for art enthusiasts. This market is renowned for its wide range of traditional Mexican handicrafts, including pottery, textiles, leather goods, and intricate silver jewelry. Don't forget to bargain while exploring the stalls, as it is a common practice in Mexican markets.

2. Paseo de la Reforma, Mexico City:

For those seeking a high-end shopping experience, Paseo de la Reforma in Mexico City is the place to be. This iconic avenue is lined with luxurious boutiques, international designer stores, and upscale shopping malls. Whether you're looking for trendy fashion, fine jewelry, or exclusive home decor, Paseo de la Reforma has it all.

3. Mercado de Sonora, Mexico City:

If you're interested in experiencing the mystical side of Mexico, head to Mercado de Sonora. This market specializes in selling traditional Mexican folk art, religious artifacts, herbs, and even live animals used in spiritual rituals. It's a unique place to immerse yourself in the enchanting world of Mexican mysticism.

4. Zona Rosa, Mexico City:

Zona Rosa is a vibrant neighborhood in Mexico City known for its lively atmosphere and diverse shopping options. Here, you'll find a mix of trendy fashion boutiques, antique shops, art galleries, and quirky souvenir stores. Take a leisurely stroll along the streets of Zona Rosa and discover unique treasures to take home.

5. San Miguel de Allende:

Recognized as a UNESCO World Heritage site, San Miguel de Allende is not only famous for its colonial architecture but also for its thriving arts and crafts scene. The town is dotted with art galleries, artisan workshops, and boutique stores selling handmade goods such as ceramics, textiles, and silverware. Don't miss the local markets, where you can find authentic Mexican crafts at reasonable prices.

6. Oaxaca City:

Oaxaca City is a vibrant cultural hub known for its indigenous traditions and vibrant markets. The Mercado de Benito Juárez is a must-visit, offering an incredible array of local specialties such as colorful textiles, hand-carved wooden figurines, and intricately designed pottery. Additionally, the Mercado 20 de Noviembre is famous for its delicious food stalls, where you can savor traditional Oaxacan cuisine.

Conclusion:

Shopping in Mexico is an adventure in itself, offering a wide range of unique and authentic treasures. Whether you're interested in traditional crafts, contemporary fashion, or spiritual artifacts, Mexico has something for everyone. Remember to explore the local markets, engage with artisans, and embrace the vibrant culture while indulging in a shopping spree. Happy shopping!,

# Chapter 24: Nightlife in Mexico

Introduction:

Mexico is renowned for its vibrant and energetic nightlife, offering visitors an unforgettable experience after the sun sets. From bustling cities to beachside towns, Mexico boasts a diverse range of venues and activities that cater to every taste and preference. This chapter will guide you through some of the best places to go out at night in Mexico, along with valuable tips for fully enjoying the country's captivating nightlife.

1. Mexico City: A Nightlife Paradise

Mexico City, the country's capital, is a thriving hub of nightlife that caters to all tastes. From trendy nightclubs to traditional cantinas, the city offers a plethora of options for an unforgettable night out. Head to the trendy neighborhoods of Polanco and Condesa, where you'll find an array of upscale bars and clubs. For a taste of authentic Mexican nightlife, visit the traditional cantinas in the historic center, where you can enjoy live music, mezcal, and delicious local cuisine.

2. Cancun: The Party Capital

Cancun is internationally renowned for its vibrant party scene, attracting millions of visitors each year. The Hotel Zone is the epicenter of Cancun's nightlife, with numerous bars, clubs, and beachside parties that continue until dawn. For an unforgettable experience, visit Coco Bongo, a world-famous nightclub known for its extravagant shows and lively atmosphere. Additionally, Isla Mujeres, a short ferry ride away, offers a more laid-back nightlife experience with beachfront bars and live music.

3. Playa del Carmen: A Mix of Laid-Back and Lively

Playa del Carmen, located in the Riviera Maya, strikes the perfect balance between a relaxed beach town and a vibrant nightlife destination. Fifth Avenue, the city's main street, is lined with bars, clubs, and restaurants, offering a diverse range of options for a night out. For a unique experience, visit La Santanera, a multi-level nightclub known for its eclectic music and vibrant atmosphere. If you prefer a more laid-back evening, head to one of the beachfront bars where you can enjoy a refreshing drink while listening to the sound of the waves.

4. Guadalajara: The Birthplace of Mariachi

Guadalajara, the capital of Jalisco, is known as the birthplace of mariachi music and tequila. The city's nightlife revolves around the traditional cantinas, where you can immerse yourself in the lively atmosphere while enjoying live mariachi performances. For a more contemporary experience, visit the Chapultepec neighborhood, known for its trendy bars, clubs, and live music venues. Don't forget to try the local tequila and raicilla, a traditional Mexican spirit, to truly embrace the spirit of Guadalajara's nightlife.

Tips for Enjoying the Nightlife in Mexico:

1. Safety first: While Mexico offers an incredible nightlife experience, it's essential to prioritize your safety. Stick to well-lit and populated areas, travel in groups, and be cautious with your belongings.

2. Dress code: Many nightclubs and upscale bars in Mexico have specific dress codes, so it's advisable to dress smartly to ensure entry. However, beach towns like Playa del Carmen have a more relaxed dress code, allowing for a casual beachwear style.

3. Transportation: Plan your transportation in advance, especially if you're exploring nightlife outside your accommodation area. Use reputable taxi services or rideshare apps to ensure a safe journey back to your hotel.

4. Embrace local customs: Mexican nightlife often involves live music, dancing, and socializing. Don't be afraid to join in the festivities, learn a few salsa moves, or try traditional Mexican drinks and cuisine.

Conclusion:

Mexico's nightlife offers a kaleidoscope of experiences, from lively nightclubs to traditional cantinas and beachside bars. Whether you're seeking a high-energy party or a relaxed evening by the shore, Mexico has something for everyone. Remember to prioritize safety, embrace local customs, and indulge in the vibrant atmosphere that makes Mexico's nightlife truly unique.,

# Chapter 25: Festivals and Events in Mexico

Introduction:

Mexico is a vibrant and culturally rich country that celebrates numerous festivals and events throughout the year. From traditional religious ceremonies to lively music and dance festivals, there is always something exciting happening in Mexico. In this chapter, we will explore some of the major festivals and events that take place across the country, offering you a glimpse into the diverse and colorful culture of Mexico.

1. Day of the Dead (Día de los Muertos):

One of Mexico's most iconic and internationally recognized festivals is the Day of the Dead. Celebrated on November 1st and 2nd, this festival honors deceased loved ones and is a unique blend of indigenous traditions and Catholicism. Families create elaborate altars adorned with marigolds, photographs, and the favorite foods and drinks of the departed. It is a time of remembrance, celebration, and reconnecting with the spirits of the deceased.

2. Guelaguetza Festival:

The Guelaguetza Festival, held annually in the city of Oaxaca, is a colorful celebration of indigenous cultures from the region. Taking place in July, this festival showcases traditional dances, music, and costumes from various communities. The highlight of the event is the Lunes del Cerro (Mondays on the Hill) performance, where dancers from different regions come together to display their cultural heritage. It is a captivating spectacle that truly represents the diversity of Mexico.

3. Carnival of Veracruz:

The Carnival of Veracruz is one of the biggest and most lively carnivals in Mexico. Held in the coastal city of Veracruz, this carnival takes place in February and lasts for nine days. The streets come alive with parades, music, dancing, and vibrant costumes. The main event is the crowning of the Carnival King and Queen, who lead the festivities throughout the city. It is a time of joy, merriment, and non-stop celebration.

4. Independence Day (Día de la Independencia):

On September 16th, Mexicans commemorate their independence from Spanish rule with great fervor and pride. The celebrations begin on the evening of September 15th, known as the Grito de Dolores (Cry of Dolores). The President of Mexico reenacts the call to arms made by Miguel Hidalgo, one of the heroes of the independence movement. Fireworks, parades, concerts, and traditional food are all part of the festivities, creating a patriotic atmosphere across the nation.

5. Festival Internacional Cervantino:

The Festival Internacional Cervantino, held in the colonial city of Guanajuato, is one of the most important cultural events in Mexico. Taking place in October, this festival celebrates the arts, particularly theater, music, dance, and visual arts. Artists from around the world come together to showcase their talents, offering a diverse range of performances and exhibitions. The historic streets and theaters of Guanajuato become a stage for creativity and artistic expression.

Conclusion:

Mexico's festival calendar is filled with an array of vibrant and significant events that reflect the country's rich cultural heritage. From the mystical Day of the Dead to the energetic Carnival of Veracruz, these festivals provide a unique opportunity to immerse yourself in the traditions, music, dance, and flavors of Mexico. As you plan your visit, be sure to check the dates of these festivals and events, as they will undoubtedly enhance your experience and create lasting memories of your time in Mexico.,

# Chapter 26: Activities for Couples in Mexico

Introduction:

Mexico, with its breathtaking landscapes, vibrant culture, and warm hospitality, is the perfect destination for couples seeking an unforgettable romantic getaway. From serene beaches to ancient ruins, Mexico offers a plethora of activities that cater to every couple's desires. In this chapter, we will explore the top 10 most romantic activities for couples in Mexico, ensuring a truly memorable experience filled with love and adventure.

1. Sunset Stroll along Tulum Beach:

Begin your romantic journey with a leisurely sunset stroll along the pristine shores of Tulum Beach. As the golden rays of the sun paint the sky in hues of orange and pink, hand in hand with your loved one, relish the serenity and tranquility of this breathtaking setting.

2. Hot Air Balloon Ride over Teotihuacan:

Embark on a magical hot air balloon ride over the ancient ruins of Teotihuacan. As you soar above the mysterious pyramids and temples, witness the awe-inspiring beauty of this UNESCO World Heritage site. The peacefulness of the skies combined with the historical grandeur below will create an unforgettable memory for you and your partner.

3. Romantic Dinner Cruise in Cancun:

Indulge in a romantic dinner cruise along the stunning coastline of Cancun. As you sail under the starlit sky, savor a delectable gourmet meal and toast to your love. The gentle sway of the boat, the sound of the waves, and the enchanting views will transport you to a world of pure romance.

4. Couples' Spa Retreat in San Miguel de Allende:

Pamper yourselves with a rejuvenating couples' spa retreat in the charming town of San Miguel de Allende. Unwind in luxurious spas, where skilled therapists will massage away your stress and revitalize your senses. The tranquil ambiance and the healing treatments will leave you feeling connected and refreshed.

5. Horseback Riding in Valle de Guadalupe:

Escape to the picturesque wine region of Valle de Guadalupe and embark on a romantic horseback ride through rolling vineyards. As you explore this idyllic landscape, take in the breathtaking views of the valley and savor the exquisite flavors of local wines during a private tasting.

6. Snorkeling in Cozumel:

Discover the vibrant underwater world of Cozumel hand in hand with your loved one. Dive into crystal-clear waters and explore colorful coral reefs teeming with tropical fish. The sense of adventure and the shared excitement of discovering the hidden treasures beneath the surface will create lasting memories.

7. Moonlit Mayan Ruins in Chichen Itza:

Experience the mystical allure of Chichen Itza, one of the New Seven Wonders of the World, under the moonlight. Take a guided tour of the ancient Mayan ruins, where you'll learn about their fascinating history and legends. As the moon casts an ethereal glow over the ruins, you and your partner will be transported to a bygone era.

8. Cooking Class in Oaxaca:

Ignite your culinary passions with a cooking class in the vibrant city of Oaxaca. Learn to prepare traditional Mexican dishes side by side with your partner, using fresh ingredients and age-old techniques. The shared experience of creating a delicious meal together will surely enhance your bond.

9. Whale Watching in Los Cabos:

Embark on an awe-inspiring whale-watching adventure in Los Cabos. Witness the majestic beauty of humpback whales as they breach and frolic in the sea. The sheer size and grace of these magnificent creatures will leave you and your loved one in awe of nature's wonders.

10. Private Beach Picnic in Playa del Carmen:

Escape to a secluded beach in Playa del Carmen and indulge in a private picnic for two. Bask in the sun, feel the sand between your toes, and savor a gourmet picnic basket filled with local delicacies. The privacy and intimacy of this experience will create cherished memories that will last a lifetime.

Conclusion:

Mexico offers an array of romantic activities that cater to every couple's desires. From serene beaches to ancient ruins, from culinary adventures to breathtaking landscapes, Mexico has it all. Embark on these top 10 most romantic activities for couples in Mexico, and let the magic of this vibrant country ignite the flames of love and create memories that will be cherished forever.,

# Chapter 27: Activities for Solo Travelers in Mexico

Introduction:

Mexico is a vibrant and diverse country that offers plenty of exciting opportunities for solo travelers. Whether you are seeking adventure, cultural exploration, or relaxation, Mexico has something for everyone. In this chapter, we will explore the top 10 activities that are perfect for solo travelers in Mexico. These activities will not only provide you with an unforgettable experience but also allow you to immerse yourself in the rich history and traditions of this beautiful country.

1. Explore the Ancient Mayan Ruins:

Mexico is home to some of the most impressive ancient ruins in the world. Solo travelers can visit iconic sites such as Chichen Itza, Tulum, and Palenque. Wander through the remnants of ancient civilizations, marvel at the intricate architecture, and learn about the fascinating history of the Mayan people.

2. Take a Cooking Class:

Mexican cuisine is renowned worldwide for its bold flavors and unique ingredients. As a solo traveler, why not take a cooking class and learn how to make traditional Mexican dishes? Not only will you get to savor the delicious food, but you will also gain insights into the local culture and culinary traditions.

3. Explore Mexico City:

Mexico City is a bustling metropolis that offers endless opportunities for solo travelers. Explore the historic center, visit world-class museums such as the Frida Kahlo Museum and the National Museum of Anthropology, and indulge in the vibrant street food scene. Don't forget to take a leisurely stroll through Chapultepec Park, one of the largest urban parks in the world.

4. Discover the Magic of Oaxaca:

Oaxaca is a charming city known for its rich indigenous culture and vibrant arts scene. Solo travelers can explore the colorful markets, visit the impressive Santo Domingo Church, and indulge in the local cuisine, including the famous mole sauce. Don't miss the opportunity to witness traditional Zapotec weavers creating intricate textiles.

5. Dive into the Crystal Clear Cenotes:

Mexico's Yucatan Peninsula is dotted with breathtaking cenotes, natural sinkholes filled with crystal clear freshwater. Solo travelers can take a refreshing swim in these magical underwater caves, snorkel among colorful fish, or even try their hand at scuba diving. The cenotes offer a unique and unforgettable experience for nature lovers.

6. Embark on a Whale Watching Adventure:

If you are a nature enthusiast, a solo trip to Baja California Sur is a must. Witness the awe-inspiring sight of humpback whales breaching the water's surface, as well as dolphins, sea lions, and other marine life. Take a boat tour, kayak through the tranquil waters, and immerse yourself in the beauty of Mexico's Pacific coast.

7. Experience the Day of the Dead:

Mexico's Day of the Dead, or Dia de los Muertos, is a vibrant and colorful celebration of life and death. As a solo traveler, you can witness this unique tradition firsthand by visiting cities such as Oaxaca, Pátzcuaro, or Mexico City. Join the parades, marvel at the elaborate altars, and participate in the festivities to gain a deeper understanding of Mexican culture.

8. Hike the Copper Canyon:

For adventure seekers, hiking the Copper Canyon in the state of Chihuahua is an exhilarating experience. This vast and rugged canyon system offers breathtaking views, challenging trails, and encounters with indigenous Tarahumara communities. Embark on a multi-day trek, camp under the stars, and immerse yourself in the natural beauty of Mexico's wilderness.

9. Relax on the Beaches of the Riviera Maya:

Solo travelers looking for relaxation can unwind on the pristine beaches of the Riviera Maya. From the famous Playa del Carmen to the secluded Tulum, these beaches offer turquoise waters, white sand, and a laid-back atmosphere. Soak up the sun, snorkel in the coral reefs, or simply enjoy a tranquil beachside yoga session.

10. Attend a Lucha Libre Match:

For a unique and entertaining experience, catch a Lucha Libre match in Mexico City. This Mexican style of professional wrestling is known for its colorful masks, acrobatic moves, and lively atmosphere. Join the cheering crowd, immerse yourself in the excitement, and witness this beloved Mexican tradition firsthand.

Conclusion:

Mexico is a solo traveler's paradise, offering a wide range of activities that cater to different interests and preferences. From exploring ancient ruins to indulging in delicious cuisine, Mexico has it all. So, pack your bags, embrace the spirit of adventure, and embark on an unforgettable journey through this enchanting country.,

# Chapter 28: Budget-friendly activities in Mexico

Introduction:

Mexico is a vibrant and culturally rich country that offers a wide range of activities for budget-conscious travelers. From exploring ancient ruins to indulging in delicious street food, there are plenty of affordable options to make the most of your trip. In this chapter, we will delve into the top 10 budget-friendly activities that will allow you to experience the best of Mexico without breaking the bank.

1. Explore the Mayan Ruins of Tulum:

Start your budget-friendly adventure by visiting the stunning Mayan ruins of Tulum. With its breathtaking coastal views and well-preserved structures, this archaeological site offers a fascinating glimpse into Mexico's ancient history. The entrance fee is relatively low, making it a must-visit attraction for budget travelers.

2. Wander through Mexico City's Historic Center:

Mexico City's Historic Center is a UNESCO World Heritage site and a treasure trove of history and culture. Take a leisurely stroll through its vibrant streets, marvel at the stunning architecture, and visit notable landmarks such as the Metropolitan Cathedral and the National Palace. Entrance to most of these attractions is free, allowing you to immerse yourself in the city's rich heritage without spending a fortune.

3. Enjoy the Beaches of Playa del Carmen:

For a relaxing day by the sea, head to the pristine beaches of Playa del Carmen. This popular coastal town offers crystal-clear waters, powdery white sand, and a laid-back atmosphere. You can spend the day sunbathing, swimming, or simply enjoying the breathtaking views. The best part? Access to most public beaches is free, making it an ideal budget-friendly activity.

4. Discover the Cenotes of the Yucatan Peninsula:

Mexico's Yucatan Peninsula is famous for its cenotes, natural sinkholes filled with crystal-clear water. These unique formations offer a refreshing escape from the heat and provide the perfect setting for snorkeling or swimming. Many cenotes have affordable entrance fees, and some even offer discounts if you bring your own snorkeling gear.

5. Sample Street Food in Mexico City:

One of the best ways to experience Mexico's culinary delights without breaking the bank is by indulging in the street food scene of Mexico City. From tacos and quesadillas to tamales and elotes, the options are endless. Wander through the bustling markets and street stalls, savoring the flavors of authentic Mexican cuisine at incredibly affordable prices.

6. Hike to the Sumidero Canyon in Chiapas:

Nature lovers will be delighted by the stunning Sumidero Canyon in Chiapas. Take a boat tour along the Grijalva River and marvel at the towering cliffs and abundant wildlife. The entrance fee for the boat tour is budget-friendly, and the experience is truly unforgettable.

7. Visit the Frida Kahlo Museum in Mexico City:

Immerse yourself in the life and art of one of Mexico's most iconic figures, Frida Kahlo, at her former home turned museum. The Frida Kahlo Museum, also known as the Blue House, showcases her personal belongings and artwork. The entrance fee is reasonable, allowing you to gain insight into the life of this legendary artist without breaking the bank.

8. Explore the Colorful Town of Guanajuato:

Guanajuato is a picturesque colonial town known for its vibrant colors and charming streets. Spend a day wandering through its narrow alleyways, admiring the stunning architecture, and soaking up the lively atmosphere. Many of the town's attractions, such as the famous Callejón del Beso (Alley of the Kiss), can be explored for free.

9. Discover the Magic of Oaxaca's Markets:

Oaxaca is renowned for its vibrant markets, where you can find an array of traditional crafts, textiles, and local delicacies. Explore the bustling Mercado Benito Juarez or the Mercado 20 de Noviembre, where you can sample delicious regional dishes at affordable prices. The markets offer a unique cultural experience and are a budget-friendly way to immerse yourself in the local culture.

10. Relax in the Hot Springs of Hierve el Agua:

Escape the crowds and unwind in the natural mineral-rich pools of Hierve el Agua. Located in the Oaxaca region, these stunning petrified waterfalls offer a tranquil setting to relax and rejuvenate. The entrance fee is minimal, making it an excellent budget-friendly activity for nature enthusiasts.

Conclusion:

Mexico provides a plethora of budget-friendly activities that allow travelers to experience the country's rich history, vibrant culture, and natural beauty without breaking the bank. From exploring ancient ruins and indulging in street food to discovering picturesque towns and relaxing in natural wonders, Mexico offers something for every budget-conscious traveler. Embrace the spirit of adventure and make the most of your trip by enjoying these affordable activities while creating unforgettable memories.,

# Chapter 29: Off-the-beaten-path activities in Mexico

Introduction:

Mexico is a country that offers countless opportunities for exploration and adventure. While popular tourist destinations like Cancun, Mexico City, and Tulum attract large crowds, there are hidden gems scattered throughout the country that are still relatively undiscovered by tourists. In this chapter, we will uncover the top 10 off-the-beaten-path activities in Mexico, allowing you to experience the country's authentic culture, breathtaking landscapes, and unique adventures.

1. Exploring the Cenotes of the Yucatan Peninsula:

Escape the crowded beaches of the Riviera Maya and head to the Yucatan Peninsula, where an intricate network of cenotes awaits. These natural sinkholes, filled with crystal-clear turquoise water, offer a surreal swimming experience. Dive into the depths of these cenotes, explore their underwater caves, and even snorkel alongside ancient Mayan artifacts.

2. Discovering the Magic of San Cristobal de las Casas:

Nestled in the highlands of Chiapas, San Cristobal de las Casas is a charming colonial town with a vibrant indigenous culture. Stroll through its narrow cobblestone streets, visit local markets, and immerse yourself in the rich traditions of the indigenous communities. Don't miss the opportunity to witness traditional Mayan ceremonies and explore nearby indigenous villages.

3. Hiking in Copper Canyon:

Often referred to as Mexico's version of the Grand Canyon, Copper Canyon is a hidden natural wonder in the state of Chihuahua. Embark on a multi-day hiking adventure through its rugged terrain, crossing suspension bridges, and witnessing breathtaking panoramic views. Encounter indigenous Tarahumara communities along the way and learn about their fascinating way of life.

4. Snorkeling with Whale Sharks in Isla Holbox:

Escape the crowded tourist spots and head to Isla Holbox, a tranquil island off the Yucatan Peninsula. Here, you can embark on a once-in-a-lifetime experience of swimming alongside gentle giants – the whale sharks. These magnificent creatures migrate through the waters surrounding the island, providing an unforgettable snorkeling encounter.

5. Exploring the Hidden Beach of Marietas Islands:

Located off the coast of Puerto Vallarta, the Marietas Islands are home to a hidden beach known as Playa del Amor or the Beach of Love. This secluded paradise can only be accessed by swimming through a long tunnel. Once you emerge, you'll find yourself surrounded by a pristine beach nestled within a collapsed volcanic crater.

6. Visiting the Surreal Sculptures of Edward James' Las Pozas:

In the heart of the Mexican jungle, near Xilitla, lies a surreal wonderland created by the eccentric British artist Edward James. Las Pozas, meaning the Pools in Spanish, is a collection of whimsical sculptures and structures that blend seamlessly with the surrounding natural landscape. Explore this hidden gem and let your imagination run wild.

7. Experiencing the Magic of Hierve el Agua:

Located in the state of Oaxaca, Hierve el Agua is a natural wonder that will leave you in awe. These petrified waterfalls were created by mineral-rich springs over thousands of years. Take a dip in the natural infinity pools, hike through the surrounding trails, and witness the stunning panoramic views of the Oaxacan countryside.

8. Horseback Riding in the Sierra Gorda:

Escape the tourist crowds and venture into the Sierra Gorda Biosphere Reserve in Queretaro. Explore this hidden gem on horseback, riding through lush forests, crossing rivers, and discovering hidden waterfalls. Immerse yourself in the tranquility of nature and witness the diverse wildlife that calls this reserve home.

9. Exploring the Caves of Cacahuamilpa:

Located in the state of Guerrero, the Caves of Cacahuamilpa are a hidden underground wonder. Embark on a guided tour through the massive caverns, adorned with impressive stalactite and stalagmite formations. Marvel at the natural beauty that lies beneath the surface and learn about the geological history of this unique attraction.

10. Discovering the Art of Mezcal in Oaxaca:

While tequila is often associated with Mexico, Oaxaca is the birthplace of another iconic Mexican spirit – Mezcal. Escape the touristy tequila tours and head to Oaxaca to explore the traditional mezcal distilleries. Learn about the intricate process of producing this smoky and flavorful spirit, and of course, indulge in tastings of various mezcal varieties.

Conclusion:

Mexico's off-the-beaten-path activities offer a chance to escape the crowds and delve deeper into the country's rich cultural and natural wonders. From exploring hidden cenotes to discovering surreal sculptures and embarking on unique wildlife encounters, these experiences will provide you with memories that will last a lifetime. Step off the well-trodden path and immerse yourself in the authentic and lesser-known side of Mexico.,

# Chapter 30: Sustainable Tourism Experiences in Mexico

Introduction:

Mexico is a country rich in natural and cultural wonders, offering a wide range of sustainable tourism experiences for visitors. In this chapter, we will explore the top 10 sustainable tourism experiences in Mexico, where travelers can immerse themselves in the country's beauty while supporting conservation efforts and local communities.

1. Exploring the Sian Ka'an Biosphere Reserve:

Located on the Yucatan Peninsula, Sian Ka'an is a UNESCO World Heritage Site and one of Mexico's largest protected areas. Travelers can embark on guided tours to witness its diverse ecosystems, including mangroves, wetlands, and coral reefs. Through sustainable practices, such as low-impact tourism and community involvement, Sian Ka'an ensures the preservation of its natural treasures.

2. Volunteering at a Sea Turtle Conservation Project:

Mexico's coastline is home to several sea turtle nesting sites, offering visitors the chance to actively participate in conservation efforts. Joining a volunteer program allows travelers to assist in protecting turtle nests, releasing hatchlings, and educating local communities about the importance of preserving these endangered species.

3. Exploring the Copper Canyon:

The Copper Canyon, located in the Sierra Madre Occidental, is a stunning natural wonder that rivals the Grand Canyon in the United States. To experience this breathtaking landscape sustainably, travelers can opt for eco-friendly train rides, hiking tours, or biking excursions, all of which minimize the ecological impact on this fragile ecosystem.

4. Visiting the Calakmul Biosphere Reserve:

Situated in the southern state of Campeche, the Calakmul Biosphere Reserve is home to an impressive array of flora and fauna, including jaguars, howler monkeys, and countless bird species. By visiting this reserve, travelers contribute to its conservation efforts while enjoying guided tours, birdwatching, and exploring ancient Mayan ruins.

5. Engaging in Community-Based Tourism in Chiapas:

In the southern state of Chiapas, various indigenous communities have embraced sustainable tourism as a means of preserving their cultural heritage. Travelers can stay in community-run eco-lodges, participate in traditional activities, and learn about the customs and traditions of these communities, all while supporting local economies and fostering cultural exchange.

6. Discovering the Whale Sharks of Isla Holbox:

Isla Holbox, located off the Yucatan Peninsula, is renowned for its annual gathering of whale sharks, the largest fish in the world. Responsible tourism practices, such as swimming with these gentle giants under the guidance of knowledgeable guides, ensure minimal disturbance to their natural habitat and promote conservation awareness.

7. Exploring the Biosphere Reserve of Ria Lagartos:

Ria Lagartos, in the state of Yucatan, is a haven for wildlife enthusiasts. This biosphere reserve offers sustainable tourism experiences, such as birdwatching tours, kayaking through mangroves, and observing nesting flamingos. By supporting local guides and their conservation efforts, visitors contribute to the protection of this fragile ecosystem.

8. Participating in Agroecotourism in Oaxaca:

The state of Oaxaca is known for its rich cultural heritage and diverse landscapes. Travelers can engage in agroecotourism experiences, such as visiting organic coffee farms, learning about traditional farming practices, and enjoying farm-to-table culinary experiences. These sustainable activities support local farmers and promote sustainable agriculture.

9. Discovering the Underwater Museum in Cancun:

The Cancun Underwater Museum (MUSA) is an innovative project that combines art and conservation. Travelers can explore the underwater sculptures created by renowned artists, which serve as artificial reefs, promoting the growth of marine life and relieving pressure on natural coral reefs. Snorkeling or diving in this unique museum supports marine conservation efforts.

10. Experiencing Sustainable Luxury in Riviera Maya:

Riviera Maya offers sustainable luxury accommodations that prioritize eco-friendly practices and community engagement. Travelers can enjoy high-end resorts that implement sustainable initiatives, such as renewable energy, waste reduction, and support for local artisans. By choosing sustainable luxury, visitors contribute to the preservation of Mexico's natural beauty while enjoying a luxurious vacation.

Conclusion:

Mexico's commitment to sustainable tourism ensures that visitors can experience the country's wonders while actively supporting conservation efforts and local communities. By engaging in the top 10 sustainable tourism experiences highlighted in this chapter, travelers not only create unforgettable memories but also contribute to the long-term preservation of Mexico's natural and cultural heritage.,

# Chapter 31: Responsible Tourism Experiences in Mexico

Introduction:

Mexico, a vibrant and diverse country, offers a plethora of responsible tourism experiences that not only allow travelers to explore its rich culture and natural wonders but also contribute towards the well-being of local communities and preservation of the environment. In this chapter, we will delve into the top 10 responsible tourism experiences in Mexico, providing you with unique and truthful insights to make your visit an unforgettable and meaningful one.

1. Volunteering with Local Conservation Projects:

Immerse yourself in the breathtaking natural landscapes of Mexico by participating in local conservation projects. From sea turtle conservation in the Riviera Maya to whale watching and marine research in Baja California, these initiatives allow you to contribute to the preservation of Mexico's diverse flora and fauna while learning from passionate experts.

2. Exploring Indigenous Communities:

Embark on a journey to discover the rich cultural heritage of Mexico's indigenous communities. Engage in authentic experiences, such as learning traditional crafts, participating in ancient rituals, and tasting local cuisine. By supporting these communities through responsible tourism, you contribute to their economic empowerment and cultural preservation.

3. Sustainable Farming and Agro-Tourism:

Mexico's agricultural traditions are deeply rooted in its history. Experience the beauty of sustainable farming practices by visiting organic farms and participating in hands-on activities like harvesting crops, making traditional dishes, and learning about agro-ecological techniques. This responsible tourism experience not only supports local farmers but also promotes sustainable food production.

4. Eco-Friendly Adventure Tourism:

Mexico's diverse geography offers countless opportunities for eco-friendly adventure tourism. Whether it's exploring the underground rivers of the Yucatan Peninsula, hiking in the Copper Canyon, or snorkeling in the crystal-clear waters of the Riviera Nayarit, responsible tour operators ensure minimal impact on the environment while providing thrilling experiences for travelers.

5. Community-Based Tourism:

Engage with local communities through community-based tourism initiatives. Stay in eco-lodges run by indigenous families, participate in cultural exchange programs, and learn about traditional practices, such as handicrafts and cooking. By choosing community-based tourism, you directly contribute to the economic development of these communities and help preserve their cultural heritage.

6. Responsible Wildlife Encounters:

Mexico is home to an astonishing array of wildlife, including jaguars, monkeys, and colorful bird species. Opt for responsible wildlife encounters by visiting reputable sanctuaries and reserves that prioritize animal welfare and conservation efforts. Learn about the importance of protecting these species and contribute to their preservation through responsible tourism practices.

7. Sustainable Coastal Tourism:

Mexico's stunning coastlines attract millions of tourists each year. Choose sustainable coastal tourism options that prioritize the protection of marine ecosystems. Engage in activities like responsible snorkeling, beach clean-ups, and supporting local initiatives that aim to reduce plastic pollution and promote sustainable fishing practices.

8. Cultural Heritage Preservation:

Mexico's cultural heritage is a treasure trove of ancient civilizations. Visit archaeological sites like Chichen Itza, Teotihuacan, and Palenque, and support responsible tourism practices that prioritize the preservation and respectful exploration of these historical landmarks. By doing so, you contribute to the ongoing conservation efforts and ensure future generations can appreciate Mexico's rich history.

9. Responsible Food Tourism:

Mexico's culinary traditions are renowned worldwide. Engage in responsible food tourism by choosing local restaurants and street food vendors that prioritize sustainable sourcing, support small-scale producers, and promote traditional cooking techniques. By indulging in Mexico's gastronomic delights, you support responsible practices that benefit local communities and the environment.

10. Conservation-focused Accommodations:

Choose accommodations that prioritize sustainability and conservation. From eco-lodges nestled in the jungles to boutique hotels committed to reducing their carbon footprint, these establishments offer responsible tourism experiences that align with your values. By staying in these accommodations, you directly contribute to environmental preservation and support local communities.

Conclusion:

By engaging in responsible tourism experiences in Mexico, you have the power to make a positive impact on the environment, local communities, and cultural heritage. From volunteering with conservation projects to supporting indigenous communities and choosing sustainable options, each responsible choice you make contributes towards a more sustainable and inclusive future for Mexico's tourism industry. Embrace these unique and truthful experiences, and let your journey through Mexico be one of responsible exploration and meaningful connections.,

# Chapter 32: Volunteer Opportunities in Mexico

Introduction:

Mexico is not only known for its stunning beaches, rich culture, and delicious cuisine, but it also offers incredible opportunities for travelers to make a positive impact through volunteering. Whether you're passionate about conservation, education, or community development, Mexico has a wide range of volunteer programs that allow you to immerse yourself in the local culture while giving back to the community. In this chapter, we will explore the top 10 volunteer opportunities in Mexico, providing you with unique and truthful insights into each program.

1. Marine Conservation in Baja California:

Embark on a journey to protect the marine life in Baja California. Join local organizations in their efforts to preserve the delicate ecosystems, such as coral reefs and sea turtle nesting grounds. You'll have the opportunity to participate in research, beach clean-ups, and educational initiatives, all while enjoying the breathtaking beauty of the Sea of Cortez.

2. Teaching English in Oaxaca:

If you have a passion for education, consider volunteering in Oaxaca to teach English to local children. Many schools and organizations in this region offer volunteer programs that aim to improve English language skills and provide a brighter future for the children. This opportunity allows you to make a lasting impact on the lives of young students while experiencing the vibrant culture of Oaxaca.

3. Sustainable Agriculture in Chiapas:

Immerse yourself in the lush landscapes of Chiapas and contribute to sustainable agriculture practices. Work alongside local farmers, learning traditional techniques and promoting organic farming methods. This volunteer opportunity not only helps preserve the region's biodiversity but also supports local communities in achieving food security and economic stability.

4. Animal Rescue in Mexico City:

Animal lovers can make a difference by volunteering at various animal rescue centers in Mexico City. Assist in the care and rehabilitation of abandoned or mistreated animals, including dogs, cats, and even exotic species. Through your dedication, you can help provide a second chance for these animals and promote responsible pet ownership.

5. Community Development in Yucatan:

Experience the warmth and hospitality of the Yucatan Peninsula while contributing to community development projects. Volunteer in rural villages, assisting with infrastructure improvements, educational initiatives, and healthcare programs. Engage with local communities, learn about their rich cultural heritage, and leave a lasting impact on their lives.

6. Environmental Conservation in the Riviera Maya:

The Riviera Maya is not only a popular tourist destination but also a region of immense ecological importance. Join local conservation organizations to protect the diverse ecosystems, including coral reefs and mangroves. Participate in reef restoration, beach clean-ups, and educational campaigns to raise awareness about sustainable tourism practices.

7. Healthcare Support in Guadalajara:

If you have a background in healthcare or a desire to assist those in need, consider volunteering in Guadalajara. Join medical clinics and hospitals to provide much-needed support to underserved communities. Assist with basic medical procedures, health education, and outreach programs, making a tangible difference in improving people's well-being.

8. Orphanage Support in Tijuana:

Volunteer at orphanages in Tijuana and provide love, care, and support to children in need. Engage in activities that promote their emotional and educational development, such as tutoring, arts and crafts, and sports. Your time and dedication can bring joy to these children's lives and create lasting memories for both them and you.

9. Ecotourism Development in Michoacán:

Contribute to the sustainable development of ecotourism in the breathtaking landscapes of Michoacán. Work alongside local communities to create responsible tourism initiatives that preserve the region's natural beauty and cultural heritage. Help develop eco-friendly accommodations, design educational tours, and promote conservation efforts to benefit both the environment and local economies.

10. Disaster Relief in Mexico City:

In the face of natural disasters, Mexico City has often been a hub for relief efforts. Join organizations that provide support during emergencies, such as earthquakes or hurricanes. Assist in rescue operations, distribute supplies, and offer comfort to those affected. Your volunteer work during these critical times can make a significant difference in rebuilding communities and restoring hope.

Conclusion:

Mexico offers a myriad of volunteer opportunities that allow you to explore the country's diverse landscapes, immerse yourself in its vibrant culture, and make a positive impact on local communities. From marine conservation to disaster relief, each volunteer program provides a unique and truthful experience that will leave you with unforgettable memories and a sense of fulfillment. Choose the opportunity that resonates with your passions and embark on a journey of meaningful volunteerism in Mexico.,

# Chapter 33: Visas and Immigration Requirements for Mexico

Introduction:

Welcome to Chapter 33 of our comprehensive tourist guide on Mexico. In this chapter, we will provide you with a summary of the visa and immigration requirements for visiting Mexico. It is essential to familiarize yourself with these requirements to ensure a smooth and hassle-free entry into the country. Please note that the information provided here is accurate at the time of writing, but it is always recommended to verify the latest updates from the Mexican embassy or consulate in your home country.

1. Visa Exemptions:

Mexico offers visa exemptions to citizens of several countries for tourism and business purposes. These exemptions allow visitors to enter Mexico without a visa for a specified duration. The duration of the visa exemption varies depending on the nationality of the visitor. Some common visa-exempt countries include the United States, Canada, the European Union member countries, Japan, Australia, and New Zealand. However, it is important to note that the purpose of the visit must align with the visa exemption category, and the visitor must not exceed the maximum allowed stay.

2. Tourist Card (FMM):

For visitors who are not visa-exempt, Mexico requires the issuance of a Tourist Card, also known as the Forma Migratoria Múltiple (FMM). The FMM is a document that allows tourists to enter and stay in Mexico for up to 180 days. It can be obtained at the port of entry or through various Mexican consulates and embassies worldwide. The FMM must be completed accurately, and a fee may be applicable, depending on the visitor's nationality. It is crucial to retain the FMM throughout the stay in Mexico, as it must be presented upon departure.

3. Temporary Resident Visa:

For individuals planning to stay in Mexico for longer than 180 days, a Temporary Resident Visa is required. This visa is suitable for those who wish to engage in activities such as studying, working, or retiring in Mexico. The Temporary Resident Visa is valid for up to four years and can be renewed. To obtain this visa, applicants must meet specific requirements, including proof of financial solvency, a clean criminal record, and a valid passport. It is advisable to consult the nearest Mexican embassy or consulate for detailed information on the application process.

4. Work Visa:

Foreign nationals intending to work in Mexico must obtain a Work Visa (Visa de Trabajo). This visa is granted to individuals who have a job offer from a Mexican employer. The employer must initiate the visa application process through the National Immigration Institute (INM) in Mexico. The Work Visa is typically valid for one year and can be renewed. It is essential to note that working in Mexico without the appropriate visa is illegal and may result in severe consequences.

5. Other Visa Categories:

Mexico offers various other visa categories, including Student Visas, Investor Visas, and Family Reunification Visas. Each category has specific requirements and procedures. Applicants should gather all necessary documentation and consult with the Mexican embassy or consulate in their home country for detailed information on these visa categories.

Conclusion:

Understanding the visa and immigration requirements for Mexico is crucial to ensure a pleasant and lawful visit to this beautiful country. Whether you are planning a short vacation or a long-term stay, it is essential to comply with the regulations set forth by the Mexican government. Remember to review the latest updates from the official sources and seek guidance from the Mexican embassy or consulate for accurate and up-to-date information. Enjoy your time in Mexico and make unforgettable memories!,

# Chapter 34: Money and Banking in Mexico

Introduction:

Welcome to Mexico! As you embark on your journey through this vibrant country, it is essential to familiarize yourself with the currency, exchange rates, ATMs, and credit cards to ensure a smooth and hassle-free financial experience. In this chapter, we will provide you with all the necessary information, allowing you to make informed decisions regarding your money while exploring the wonders of Mexico.

Currency:

The official currency of Mexico is the Mexican Peso (MXN). It is advisable to exchange your currency for pesos upon arrival to ensure you have the local currency readily available. While some establishments may accept U.S. dollars, it is always best to have pesos on hand for smaller businesses, local markets, and transportation.

Exchange Rates:

Exchange rates fluctuate daily, so it is recommended to check the rates before exchanging your money. Banks, exchange offices, and hotels are common places to convert your currency. However, be cautious of exchange offices in tourist areas, as they may charge higher fees. Banks usually offer more favorable rates, but they may have limited operating hours.

ATMs:

ATMs are widely available throughout Mexico, particularly in cities and popular tourist destinations. They are convenient for obtaining cash in the local currency. However, it is crucial to use ATMs located within banks or reputable establishments to minimize the risk of fraudulent activities. Before your trip, inform your bank of your travel plans to avoid any issues with your debit or credit cards.

Credit Cards:

Credit cards are widely accepted in most tourist areas, hotels, restaurants, and larger establishments. Major credit cards such as Visa, Mastercard, and American Express are commonly used. However, it is advisable to carry some cash for smaller establishments or places that may not accept cards. Always notify your credit card company about your travel plans to prevent any unexpected card blocks.

Banking Services:

Banks in Mexico typically operate from Monday to Friday, between 9:00 AM and 4:00 PM. Some banks may also open on Saturdays for limited hours. It is important to carry your passport or a valid identification document when visiting a bank. Banks provide a range of services, including currency exchange, cash withdrawals, and assistance with traveler's checks.

Safety Tips:

To ensure the safety of your money and banking transactions, it is recommended to:

1. Avoid displaying large amounts of cash in public.

2. Use ATMs located within well-lit areas or inside banks.

3. Shield your PIN when entering it at ATMs.

4. Keep an eye on your credit card during transactions to prevent skimming.

5. Use reputable exchange offices or banks for currency exchange.

Conclusion:

Understanding the ins and outs of money and banking in Mexico will undoubtedly enhance your travel experience. By familiarizing yourself with the local currency, exchange rates, ATMs, and credit card usage, you can confidently navigate the financial aspects of your journey. Remember to prioritize safety and make informed decisions to make the most of your time in this beautiful country. Safe travels and enjoy your stay in Mexico!,

# Chapter 35: Communication in Mexico

Introduction:

Mexico, a vibrant and diverse country, welcomes millions of tourists each year with its rich cultural heritage and breathtaking landscapes. To ensure a smooth and connected experience during your visit, it is essential to understand the communication systems available in the country. In this chapter, we will explore the phone system, internet access, and postal service in Mexico, providing you with valuable information to stay connected while exploring this beautiful nation.

1. Phone System:

Mexico boasts a well-developed phone system that allows visitors to stay connected with their loved ones or business associates. The country's main telecommunications companies, such as Telmex, offer reliable services for both local and international calls. To make calls within Mexico, simply dial the area code followed by the local number. If you need to make international calls, dial the country code, followed by the area code and the local number. It is advisable to check with your service provider regarding roaming charges and international calling plans to avoid high expenses.

2. Internet Access:

Staying connected online has become increasingly important for travelers. Mexico offers various options for internet access, allowing visitors to easily keep in touch and access important information. Most hotels, resorts, and cafes provide Wi-Fi facilities, ensuring that you can connect your devices and stay connected throughout your trip. Additionally, major cities and tourist destinations often have internet cafes, where you can access the internet for a small fee. If you prefer to have internet access on the go, consider purchasing a local SIM card with a data plan, which will enable you to use mobile internet services.

3. Postal Service:

In Mexico, the postal service is a reliable and efficient means of sending and receiving mail. The national postal service, known as Correos de México, operates throughout the country, ensuring that your postcards, letters, or packages reach their intended destinations. Post offices can be found in most towns and cities, and they provide a range of services, including domestic and international mail, express delivery, and registered mail. It is important to keep in mind that international mail may take longer to arrive, so plan accordingly if you need to send time-sensitive items.

Conclusion:

Communication is an essential aspect of any travel experience, and Mexico offers a range of options to keep you connected during your visit. From a reliable phone system, internet access in hotels and cafes, to a well-functioning postal service, you can rest assured that staying in touch with your loved ones or conducting business will be a breeze. Remember to check with your service provider for international calling and data plans, and consider purchasing a local SIM card for convenient internet access. With these communication tools at your disposal, you can fully immerse yourself in the wonders of Mexico while staying connected to the world.,

# Chapter 36: Health and Safety in Mexico

Introduction:

Mexico is a vibrant and diverse country, attracting millions of tourists each year with its rich history, stunning landscapes, and warm hospitality. While exploring this beautiful nation, it is essential to prioritize your health and safety. This chapter aims to provide you with a summary of common health risks and valuable safety tips to ensure a memorable and secure trip to Mexico.

1. Health Risks:

a) Food and Water Safety:

- Mexico's cuisine is renowned worldwide, but it is crucial to be cautious about food hygiene.

- Stick to reputable restaurants and ensure that your food is cooked thoroughly.

- Avoid consuming tap water and opt for bottled water or boiled water instead.

- Wash fruits and vegetables with purified water before eating.

b) Altitude Sickness:

- Mexico boasts various high-altitude destinations, such as Mexico City and Oaxaca.

- If you are not accustomed to high altitudes, take it slow upon arrival to acclimatize.

- Stay hydrated, avoid alcohol, and consider using medication prescribed by your doctor.

c) Mosquito-Borne Diseases:

- Mexico is home to mosquitoes that may transmit diseases such as dengue fever, Zika virus, and chikungunya.

- Protect yourself by using insect repellents, wearing long sleeves and pants, and staying in air-conditioned or screened accommodations.

- Consult with a healthcare professional regarding vaccinations or medications before your trip.

d) Sun Exposure:

- Mexico's sunny climate can be intense, especially in coastal areas.

- Apply sunscreen with a high SPF, wear protective clothing, and seek shade during peak hours to prevent sunburn and heatstroke.

2. Safety Tips:

a) Transportation Safety:

- Utilize licensed and reputable transportation services, such as registered taxis or recognized ride-hailing apps.

- If renting a vehicle, ensure it is from a reliable agency and familiarize yourself with local traffic laws.

b) Personal Belongings:

- Keep your valuables secure and avoid displaying expensive items openly.

- Use hotel safes for passports, cash, and other important documents.

- Be cautious in crowded areas and beware of pickpockets.

c) Emergency Services:

- Familiarize yourself with the local emergency contact numbers, including police, ambulance, and your country's embassy or consulate.

- Share your travel itinerary with a trusted person and keep them updated regularly.

d) Natural Disasters:

- Mexico is prone to earthquakes, hurricanes, and tropical storms.

- Stay informed about weather conditions and follow any instructions or evacuation orders issued by local authorities.

- If traveling during hurricane season (June to November), consider travel insurance that covers trip disruptions.

Conclusion:

By prioritizing your health and safety, you can fully enjoy the wonders Mexico has to offer. Remember to be mindful of food and water hygiene, protect yourself from mosquito bites, and take necessary precautions against sun exposure. Additionally, stay vigilant about personal belongings, utilize reliable transportation, and familiarize yourself with emergency services. By following these tips, you can ensure a safe and unforgettable experience in Mexico.,

# Chapter 37: Travel Insurance for Mexico

Introduction:

Traveling to Mexico can be an exciting and memorable experience. From the stunning beaches of Cancun to the ancient ruins of Chichen Itza, this vibrant country offers a plethora of attractions for tourists. However, it is crucial to ensure that your trip is not marred by unexpected circumstances such as accidents, illnesses, or lost belongings. This is where travel insurance comes into play. In this chapter, we will explore the benefits of travel insurance specifically tailored for Mexico, as well as provide information on how to purchase it.

Benefits of Travel Insurance for Mexico:

1. Medical Coverage: One of the primary advantages of travel insurance is the provision of medical coverage. In Mexico, medical expenses can be costly, especially for foreigners. Travel insurance ensures that you are protected in case of any unexpected illnesses or injuries during your trip. It covers hospitalization, doctor's fees, emergency medical evacuation, and medication expenses.

2. Trip Cancellation/Interruption: Travel plans can sometimes be disrupted due to unforeseen circumstances, such as natural disasters, political unrest, or personal emergencies. Travel insurance safeguards your investment by reimbursing you for non-refundable expenses, including flights, accommodations, and pre-booked activities if your trip gets canceled or cut short.

3. Lost or Delayed Baggage: Losing your luggage or experiencing delays can be a nightmare while traveling. Travel insurance for Mexico provides coverage for lost, stolen, or damaged baggage. It also compensates you for essential items you may need to purchase while waiting for your belongings to be located or replaced.

4. Emergency Assistance: Navigating unfamiliar territory can be challenging, especially during an emergency. Travel insurance offers

24/7 emergency assistance services, including access to a multilingual helpline, which can provide guidance, arrange medical appointments, or assist in case of legal issues.

5. Personal Liability: Accidents happen, and sometimes they can involve third parties. Travel insurance protects you against any legal liabilities you may face due to accidental bodily injury or property damage caused to others during your trip in Mexico.

How to Purchase Travel Insurance for Mexico:

1. Research and Compare: Start by researching different insurance providers that offer coverage specifically for Mexico. Compare their policies, coverage limits, exclusions, and customer reviews to find the best fit for your needs.

2. Determine Coverage Requirements: Assess the specific coverage you require for your trip to Mexico. Consider factors such as the duration of your stay, planned activities, and any pre-existing medical conditions. Ensure that the insurance policy you choose meets your specific needs.

3. Obtain Quotes: Contact the insurance providers you shortlisted and request quotes based on your coverage requirements. Take note of the premium costs, deductibles, and any additional fees associated with the policy.

4. Read the Fine Print: Before finalizing your decision, carefully read the policy documents, including terms and conditions, coverage exclusions, and claim procedures. Ensure that you understand the policy thoroughly to avoid any surprises later on.

5. Purchase the Policy: Once you have selected the most suitable insurance provider and policy, proceed with purchasing the travel insurance. Make sure to keep a copy of the policy documents and emergency contact details with you during your trip.

Conclusion:

Travel insurance is an essential aspect of planning your trip to Mexico. It provides peace of mind, ensuring that you are protected against unexpected events that may occur during your travels. By understanding the benefits of travel insurance and following the steps outlined in this chapter, you can make an informed decision and purchase the right coverage for your Mexican adventure. Remember, it's better to be safe than sorry!,

# Chapter 38: Learning the Language of Mexico

Introduction:

Welcome to Chapter 38 of our tourist guide, where we will explore the fascinating world of learning the language of Mexico. Mexico is a country rich in culture, history, and diversity, and by learning the local language, you can enhance your travel experience and connect with the local people on a deeper level. In this chapter, we will provide you with a summary of the resources available for learning the language of Mexico, ensuring that your language learning journey is both unique and truthful.

1. Language Schools:

Mexico is home to numerous language schools that cater to international students seeking to learn Spanish. These schools offer immersive language programs, allowing you to practice your skills in real-life situations. Some renowned language schools in Mexico include the Instituto Cervantes, the University of Guadalajara Language Center, and the Frida Spanish School. These institutions provide structured courses, experienced teachers, and cultural activities to help you grasp the language effectively.

2. Online Language Learning Platforms:

In today's digital age, online language learning platforms have become increasingly popular. Websites and mobile applications such as Duolingo, Babbel, and Rosetta Stone offer interactive language courses specifically designed for learning Spanish. These platforms provide a convenient and flexible way to learn at your own pace, with features like pronunciation exercises, vocabulary building, and interactive quizzes.

3. Language Exchange Programs:

If you prefer a more immersive and interactive learning experience, participating in language exchange programs can be a great option. These programs connect you with native Spanish speakers who are interested in learning your language. Through conversation and cultural exchange, you can improve your language skills while helping others with their language goals. Websites like

ConversationExchange.com and Tandem allow you to find language partners in Mexico who are willing to engage in language exchange.

4. Local Language Meetups:

Another excellent way to practice your language skills and meet like-minded individuals is by attending local language meetups. These events bring together language enthusiasts, both locals and foreigners, who gather to practice speaking Spanish. Meetup.com is a popular platform that allows you to find language exchange groups and social events in various cities across Mexico. By attending these meetups, you can practice your conversational skills and make new friends.

5. Language Learning Apps:

In addition to online platforms, there are several language learning apps available that can assist you in your language learning journey. Apps like Memrise, HelloTalk, and FluentU provide interactive lessons, flashcards, and authentic content such as videos and podcasts to enhance your language skills. These apps offer a convenient way to learn on the go, allowing you to practice anytime and anywhere.

Conclusion:

Learning the language of Mexico opens up a world of opportunities during your travels. By immersing yourself in the local language, you can better understand the culture, connect with the people, and navigate through the country with ease. Whether you choose to enroll in a language school, use online platforms, participate in language exchange programs, or attend local meetups, the resources available for learning Spanish in Mexico are abundant. Embrace the challenge, practice regularly, and soon you'll find yourself communicating confidently in Spanish, enriching your travel experience in this vibrant country.,

# Chapter 39: Tips for Traveling with Children in Mexico

Introduction:

Traveling with children can be an exciting and enriching experience, especially in a country as vibrant and diverse as Mexico. However, it's important to plan ahead and ensure that your trip is enjoyable for both you and your little ones. In this chapter, we will provide you with valuable tips on what to pack, where to stay, and things to do when traveling with children in Mexico.

1. Packing Essentials:

When traveling with children, it's crucial to pack all the necessary essentials to ensure a comfortable trip. Here are some items you should consider bringing:

- Sunscreen and hats: Mexico's sunny climate calls for proper sun protection.

- Insect repellent: Protect your children from pesky mosquito bites, especially in tropical areas.

- Medication and first aid kit: Carry any necessary medications your children may need, along with a basic first aid kit.

- Snacks and drinks: Pack some healthy snacks and drinks to keep your children energized during the trip.

- Comfortable clothing and shoes: Mexico's diverse landscapes may require different types of clothing, so pack accordingly.

- Entertainment: Bring books, toys, and games to keep your children entertained during long journeys.

2. Choosing Family-Friendly Accommodation:

Selecting the right accommodation is crucial when traveling with children. Consider the following factors when choosing where to stay:

- Safety: Ensure that the accommodation has safety measures in place, such as childproofing, secure locks, and a safe environment.

- Amenities: Look for family-friendly amenities like swimming pools, playgrounds, and kids' clubs to keep your children entertained.

- Location: Opt for accommodations located near family-friendly attractions, parks, or beaches for easy access to entertainment options.

- Space: Choose accommodations that offer spacious rooms or interconnected rooms to give your children ample space to move around and play.

3. Exploring Child-Friendly Destinations:

Mexico offers a myriad of child-friendly destinations that will keep your little ones entertained throughout your trip. Consider the following activities:

- Visit theme parks: Mexico boasts numerous theme parks, such as Xcaret Park and Xel-Ha, which offer an array of activities suitable for children of all ages.

- Explore archaeological sites: Take your children on an educational adventure by visiting archaeological sites like Chichen Itza or Tulum. Engage them with fascinating stories about ancient civilizations.

- Enjoy beach time: Mexico's stunning beaches are perfect for family fun. Look for beaches with calm waters and shallow areas, such as Playa del Carmen or Cancun, where your children can safely swim and build sandcastles.

- Wildlife encounters: Take your children to wildlife sanctuaries or eco-parks where they can interact with animals like dolphins, sea turtles, or monkeys.

Conclusion:

Traveling with children in Mexico can be an incredible experience, filled with adventure and cultural exploration. By following these tips, you can ensure a smooth and enjoyable trip for your entire family. Remember to prioritize safety, choose child-friendly accommodations, and plan activities that cater to your children's interests. Embrace the wonders of Mexico together and create lasting memories that your children will cherish for a lifetime.,

# Chapter 40: Tips for Traveling with Seniors in Mexico

Introduction:

Traveling with seniors can be a rewarding and memorable experience, especially when exploring the vibrant and culturally rich country of Mexico. However, it is important to plan ahead and take certain precautions to ensure a comfortable and enjoyable trip for everyone involved. In this chapter, we will provide you with valuable tips on what to pack, where to stay, and things to do while traveling with seniors in Mexico.

1. Prioritize Comfortable Accommodations:

When choosing accommodation for your trip, prioritize comfort and accessibility. Look for hotels or rental properties that offer amenities such as elevators, ramps, and ground floor rooms. Additionally, consider proximity to attractions and medical facilities to ensure convenience and peace of mind.

2. Pack Medications and Health Essentials:

It is crucial to pack all necessary medications and health essentials for seniors. Ensure an ample supply for the duration of your trip, including any prescription medications. It is also advisable to carry a list of emergency contacts, medical conditions, and allergies in case of any unforeseen circumstances.

3. Plan for Rest and Recovery:

While Mexico offers a plethora of exciting activities, it is important to plan for rest and recovery periods, especially for seniors. Consider incorporating leisurely activities such as strolling through serene gardens, visiting museums, or enjoying a relaxing day at a beachfront spa. Balancing adventure with relaxation will help ensure a rejuvenating experience for all.

4. Opt for Guided Tours:

To make the most of your trip and avoid any unnecessary stress, consider booking guided tours. These tours often provide transportation, knowledgeable guides, and pre-planned itineraries that cater to different age groups. This way, you can explore popular attractions without worrying about logistics or getting lost.

5. Stay Hydrated and Mind the Climate:

Mexico's climate can be quite diverse, so it is important to stay hydrated and protect yourself from extreme weather conditions. Seniors are particularly susceptible to heatstroke and dehydration, so encourage them to drink plenty of water, wear appropriate clothing, and seek shade during hot hours of the day.

6. Embrace Local Cuisine:

Mexican cuisine is renowned worldwide for its vibrant flavors and variety. While traveling with seniors, explore local restaurants that offer a range of options, including traditional dishes and milder flavors. Prioritize hygiene and opt for well-established eateries to ensure a safe dining experience for everyone.

7. Take Advantage of Senior Discounts:

Mexico often offers special discounts for seniors at various attractions, museums, and transportation services. Research and inquire about these discounts to make your trip more economical. Additionally, these discounts can often provide priority access or reserved seating, enhancing the overall experience.

8. Be Mindful of Accessibility:

While Mexico has made significant strides in improving accessibility, it is essential to be mindful of potential challenges. Some areas may have uneven terrain or limited accessibility features. Prioritize destinations that are known for being senior-friendly, and research accessibility options in advance to ensure a smooth travel experience.

Conclusion:

Traveling with seniors in Mexico can be an enriching experience, allowing you to create lasting memories together. By following these tips, you can ensure a comfortable and enjoyable trip for everyone involved. From prioritizing comfortable accommodations to embracing local cuisine, Mexico offers a wide range of experiences that cater to all age groups. So, pack your bags and embark on a remarkable journey through the vibrant landscapes, rich history, and warm hospitality of Mexico.,

# Chapter 41: Tips for Traveling Solo in Mexico

Introduction:

Traveling solo can be an exhilarating and life-changing experience, especially when exploring the vibrant and culturally rich country of Mexico. However, it's essential to plan your trip carefully to ensure a safe and enjoyable adventure. In this chapter, we will provide you with valuable tips on where to stay, things to do, and how to stay safe while traveling solo in Mexico.

1. Choosing the Right Accommodation:

When traveling solo, it is crucial to select accommodations that prioritize safety and security. Opt for well-established hotels with positive reviews from fellow solo travelers. Consider staying in areas that are popular among tourists, as they tend to have better security measures in place. Additionally, hostels can be an excellent choice for solo travelers, as they provide opportunities to meet like-minded individuals and offer budget-friendly options.

2. Exploring Mexico's Must-Visit Destinations:

Mexico boasts a plethora of breathtaking destinations that solo travelers shouldn't miss. Start your journey in Mexico City, where you can immerse yourself in the country's rich history by visiting the National Museum of Anthropology or exploring the ancient ruins of Teotihuacan. Experience the vibrant culture of Oaxaca, indulge in the stunning beaches of Cancun, or discover the colonial charm of San Miguel de Allende. Research and plan your itinerary to make the most of your time in Mexico.

3. Embrace the Local Culture:

One of the most rewarding aspects of solo travel is the opportunity to connect with locals and experience their culture firsthand. Mexicans are known for their warmth and hospitality, so don't hesitate to strike up conversations with locals, try authentic cuisine, and participate in cultural events. Engaging with the local community will not only enrich your travel experience but also provide you with valuable insights and lifelong memories.

4. Transportation Safety:

While exploring Mexico, it's essential to prioritize your safety when it comes to transportation. Use reputable taxi services or ride-sharing apps instead of hailing random taxis on the street. If you plan to rent a car, ensure it is from a reliable company and thoroughly inspect it before driving off. Utilize public transportation during the daytime when it is more crowded and avoid traveling alone at night, especially in unfamiliar areas.

5. Staying Safe:

As a solo traveler, it's crucial to take precautions to ensure your safety throughout your journey. Avoid displaying expensive items or large amounts of cash, as it may make you a target for theft. Stay aware of your surroundings, particularly in crowded tourist areas, and be cautious of pickpockets. Keep important documents, such as your passport and identification, securely stored in a hotel safe. Additionally, inform someone trustworthy about your daily plans and check-in with them regularly.

Conclusion:

Traveling solo in Mexico can be an extraordinary adventure filled with unforgettable experiences. By following these tips, you can ensure a safe and enjoyable journey. Remember to embrace the local culture, choose secure accommodations, plan your itinerary wisely, and prioritize your safety at all times. With these precautions in mind, you are ready to embark on a solo trip to Mexico that will leave you with cherished memories for years to come.,

# Chapter 42: Tips for Traveling on a Budget in Mexico

Introduction:

Traveling to Mexico on a budget is an exciting adventure that allows you to explore the vibrant culture, stunning landscapes, and rich history without breaking the bank. By following these tips, you can make the most of your trip while saving money along the way.

1. Affordable Accommodation:

When it comes to finding budget-friendly accommodations in Mexico, consider staying in hostels, guesthouses, or budget hotels. These options not only offer comfortable stays but also provide opportunities to meet fellow travelers and share experiences. Additionally, booking accommodations in advance or during the off-peak season can help you secure better deals and discounts.

2. Exploring Local Cuisine:

One of the best ways to save money while traveling in Mexico is to indulge in the local cuisine. Street food stalls and local markets offer delicious and authentic meals at incredibly affordable prices. From mouth-watering tacos to flavorful tamales, you can savor a variety of dishes without straining your budget. Embrace the local flavors and venture beyond touristy restaurants for an authentic culinary experience.

3. Public Transportation:

Utilizing public transportation is not only cost-effective but also allows you to immerse yourself in the local culture. Mexico has an extensive network of buses, trams, and metro systems that connect major cities and towns. Opting for public transportation over taxis or rental cars can save you a significant amount of money while providing an opportunity to interact with locals and observe the daily life of Mexico.

4. Free and Low-Cost Activities:

Mexico offers a plethora of free or low-cost activities that allow you to explore its natural beauty and cultural heritage without spending a fortune. Visit the stunning beaches of Tulum, explore the ancient ruins of Chichen Itza, or hike through the breathtaking Copper Canyon. Many museums and historical sites also offer discounted or free entry on specific days, so plan your itinerary accordingly.

5. Bargain Shopping:

When shopping for souvenirs or local handicrafts in Mexico, it's essential to practice your bargaining skills. Street markets and artisanal shops often have flexible prices, and negotiating can help you secure better deals. Remember to be respectful and polite while bargaining, as it is a customary practice in Mexico.

6. Water and Snacks:

To save money on beverages, it's advisable to carry a reusable water bottle and refill it from filtered water stations available in most cities. Avoid buying bottled water as it can quickly add up to your expenses. Similarly, carry snacks like fruits or energy bars to keep you fueled throughout the day, reducing the need for pricey meals on the go.

7. Travel Insurance:

While traveling on a budget, it's crucial not to compromise on your safety and well-being. Investing in travel insurance ensures that you are protected in case of any unforeseen circumstances, such as medical emergencies or trip cancellations. Although it may seem like an additional expense, it provides peace of mind and can save you from potential financial burdens.

Conclusion:

Traveling on a budget in Mexico doesn't mean missing out on incredible experiences. By following these tips, you can explore the country's diverse landscapes, immerse yourself in its vibrant culture, and create unforgettable memories without straining your finances. Remember, the key is to plan ahead, embrace the local lifestyle, and make savvy choices to make the most of your budget-friendly adventure in Mexico.,

# Chapter 43: Tips for Traveling Responsibly in Mexico

Introduction:

As a responsible traveler, it is important to minimize our impact on the environment and culture of the places we visit. In this chapter, we will provide you with practical tips on how to travel responsibly in Mexico, ensuring that your experience is not only enjoyable but also sustainable and respectful.

1. Respect the Local Culture:

Mexico is known for its rich cultural heritage and traditions. To travel responsibly, make an effort to learn about the local customs and traditions before your trip. Respect the local dress code, greet people with a friendly Hola, and learn a few basic Spanish phrases. By respecting the local culture, you will not only have a more authentic experience but also contribute positively to the community.

2. Support Local Businesses:

When choosing accommodations, dining options, and souvenirs, opt for locally-owned businesses. By supporting local artisans, restaurants, and accommodations, you contribute directly to the local economy, allowing communities to thrive. Additionally, try to purchase locally-made products and souvenirs, which not only support the local economy but also help preserve traditional craftsmanship.

3. Reduce Plastic Waste:

Mexico, like many other countries, faces challenges with plastic waste. As a responsible traveler, minimize your plastic consumption by carrying a reusable water bottle and saying no to single-use plastics. Many hotels and restaurants in Mexico now provide filtered water stations, making it easier for you to refill your bottle. Furthermore, consider bringing a reusable shopping bag for your purchases, reducing the need for plastic bags.

4. Conserve Water and Energy:

Mexico, particularly in certain regions, faces water scarcity issues. To travel responsibly, be mindful of your water usage. Take shorter showers, turn off taps when not in use, and report any water leaks to the hotel staff. Similarly, conserve energy by turning off lights, air conditioning, and other electronic devices when you leave your accommodation. Being conscious of your energy consumption helps reduce the strain on local resources.

5. Respect the Environment:

Mexico is blessed with stunning natural landscapes, from pristine beaches to lush jungles. When visiting these natural areas, practice responsible tourism by leaving no trace. Avoid littering, stay on designated trails, and respect wildlife by observing from a distance. If you choose to participate in activities such as snorkeling or diving, ensure you do so responsibly, following local guidelines to protect the fragile marine ecosystems.

6. Engage in Sustainable Transportation:

Consider opting for sustainable transportation options when exploring Mexico. Public transportation, such as buses or trains, not only reduces your carbon footprint but also provides an opportunity to interact with locals. If you prefer to rent a car, choose a fuel-efficient vehicle and carpool whenever possible. Additionally, explore the option of cycling or walking to nearby attractions, immersing yourself in the local culture while minimizing your impact.

Conclusion:

By following these tips for traveling responsibly in Mexico, you can have an enriching experience while minimizing your impact on the environment and culture. Remember, responsible tourism is about leaving a positive footprint, supporting local communities, and preserving the natural and cultural heritage for future generations to enjoy.,

# Don't miss out!

Visit the website below and you can sign up to receive emails whenever AVERY B. HODGES publishes a new book. There's no charge and no obligation.

https://books2read.com/r/B-A-UXUAB-GQXOC

**BOOKS 2 READ**

Connecting independent readers to independent writers.